TASTE of TEXAS

Around 300
Recipes For Down Home
Texas Cookin' ! ! !

COOK
BOOK

Edited by
Joy Moffett Angel

EAKIN PRESS ★ Austin, Texas

Table of Contents

Recipes (Alphabetized according to company name.)

vii

Foreword

The flavors of Texas food run the gamut from light, subtle and elusive to rich, robust and hearty; from agreeably mild and well-mannered to outrageously hot and spicy. But light or hearty, mild or spicy, the foods of Texas are typified by one pervasive characteristic — they are uniquely Texan.

Texas has an ethnic cuisine all its own derived from a blending of generations of Southern Anglo, Black, Mexican, Swedish, German, and even Oriental cultures — with a pinch of other ethnic flavors added to taste. By combining the boundless imagination of Texans with the bountiful harvest of Texas, we concoct some of the greatest culinary experiences known to humankind.

Texas is the second largest food producer in the United States, but is second to none in the variety of foods it produces. And yet we process only six percent of the nation's food. By fostering the development of a food processing industry in Texas, we can contribute substantially to our state's economy and create new jobs for Texans while developing new and more profitable markets for Texas farmers and ranchers.

The Texas Department of Agriculture developed the Taste of Texas program to promote food products grown and processed in Texas. Companies that participate in the program use the red, white and blue logo on their labels and packages, and retailers use it in their media and in-store advertising to help consumers identify genuine Texas products.

The goal of the program is simply: get more people to use more Texas agricultural products. This *Taste of Texas Cookbook*, with its hundreds of great recipes from many of the companies that participate in the Taste of Texas program, will certainly help achieve that goal. Enjoy!

Jim Hightower
Commissioner
Texas Department of Agriculture

PREFACE

Foods — and Texas foods especially — have always intrigued me. While my background is that of a writer, journalist and editor, in 1983, when the Taste of Texas program was initiated by Commissioner Jim Hightower, I was among the first to become a member. Today more than 400 Texas companies, large corporations, and small enthusiastic entrepreneurs such as I, participate in this most innovative and creative program. Its sole purpose is to encourage and promote the production and sale of Texas agricultural products. From fields, pastures, and orchards of the Lone Star State come the fruits, nuts, vegetables, meats, spices, beverages, and condiments that help make the Texas kitchen unique in a special way.

These hundreds of Texas products, all carrying the Taste of Texas logo, will be conveniently found in your neighborhood food market, gourmet or specialty shops, as well as your supermarket. Texas has been blessed with well-watered prairies, long growing seasons, and hundreds of native foods. Texas's first settlers were farmers and stockmen — the Spanish, the Mexicans, immigrants from the British Isles and the European continent, and in more recent years newcomers from China, Vietnam, and other faraway places from beyond the setting sun. They all added their bit to this taste of Texas, a pinch of chili here, a kolache there, even barbecue introduced by buccaneers who fed their crews on the wild Spanish cattle.

The some 300 recipes in this *Taste of Texas Cookbook* were provided by some one hundred companies whose products are marketed in Texas and over the nation. We have tried to make it easy for you to find their products. The recipes are listed in the book by companies. Cross indexes identify the companies by towns in Texas, by product uses, by type of dish for their recipe such as meats, desserts, salads, and so on. At the back of the book is a roster of the more than 400 Taste of Texas companies, with their addresses and telephone numbers for direct mail ordering. You can also use this cookbook as a traveling companion to locate unusual gourmet producers as you travel over the state.

The concept of a *Taste of Texas Cookbook* was planted when Joyce and Norris Henry, who own the Everyday Gourmet Shop in Wichita Falls, suggested that I publish a recipe in a newspaper utilizing my product which is a sweet pepper relish marketed under the *Pepper Palate* label. Why not, I thought, have a cookbook with recipes from all Taste of Texas companies.

Perhaps the germ of the idea really began in the kitchen of my mother, Marie Moffett Ferguson. Her own interest in food has always been extraordinarily inventive and imbued with enormous curiosity. She taught me fundamentals of cookery, nutrition, and — most importantly — the artistry of a well-appointed table. She was a stickler for tradition but was always ready to try the new. These pages of culinary delight, which I know she would enjoy preparing, are dedicated to her.

— JOY MOFFETT ANGEL

ACKNOWLEDGMENTS

Family, friends, and associates in the food industry have made invaluable contributions to the *Taste of Texas Cookbook*. To my mother, Marie Moffett Ferguson, I owe a debt of gratitude for not only her inspiration but years of training in her kitchen. Credit for helping initiate the concept of the book goes to my good friends, Joyce and Norris Henry of Wichita Falls.

I also give thanks to other persons without whose efforts, contributions, stimulus, or support I would not have come so far. Then there is my aunt, Pat Smith, who has also filled in my background with cooking expertise and has always been ready to provide me with whatever I needed even before I knew I needed it. My brother, Dr. Frank Moffett, who is no slouch at cooking either, coming as he does from the same background as I, takes care of the family farm details and thus has enabled me to follow these pursuits.

Others have offered me their hearth and home, their advice and support, their time and trust. Among these are Dr. and Mrs. James W. Fox, Mr. and Mrs. Danny Muller, Grady Price, Jeff Miller, and Quade Stahl, all of Austin; Juanita Camfield, Mr. and Mrs. Stephen Brown and Frank Junell, all of San Angelo; Mr. and Mrs. Marion Sweatmon of San Antonio; Jo Anne Miller and Jane Riley of Fort Worth; Henry Bowling in Terrell and Linda Jordan in Georgetown; Robert Langkop, Mr. and Mrs. Henry Fox and Mrs. G. G. Conoley in Taylor; Sally Nesman, Dr. and Mrs. Tom Galbraith, Mr. and Mrs. Frank Pal in Wichita Falls; Brenda McKnight of Hempstead; Carol and George Norris and Judy Bunch Moritz, all of Vernon. And there is my friend and partner in cooking, Christine Lease, who has contributed ideas, proofread recipes, and lived for several moons in the midst of the paper shambles that creating a book necessarily entails.

Then there are the contributors themselves, who have sent in some of the most varied and delightful recipes and food ideas. The scope of these recipes ranges from simple down-home style (such as the recipe for roast beef) to the rarified at-

xvii

mosphere of *haute cuisine*. Others are so inventive (such as the berry-steeped chocolate cake) and so outrageously different (such as the peach-glazed pork ribs), that I was forced to stop writing and go out to purchase the ingredients for those recipes and try them out immediately. And it was worth the effort.

Naturally, thanks must also go to the Texas Department of Agriculture for the input their members have given. And to my publisher Ed Eakin, an acquaintance of more years than either of us care to admit, for his immediate and unconditional response when I first talked to him about doing this book. He has helped to make this work a pleasure.

TASTE of TEXAS

Around 300
Recipes For Down Home
Texas Cookin' ! ! !

COOK BOOK

LEMON PECAN CAKE

2 cups (4 sticks) margarine,
  softened
2½ cups (1 lb.) packed light
  brown sugar
6 eggs, separated
4 cups flour
¼ tsp. salt
2 tsp. baking powder
½ cup milk
1½ oz. Adams Lemon Extract
2 cups pecans, chopped

Preheat oven to 300°. Cream margarine and sugar. Add egg yolks. Blend well. Sift flour, salt and baking powder together. Add flour mixture alternately with milk. Add Adams Lemon Extract and pecans. Mix until well blended. Beat egg whites to peak. Fold into batter. Pour into a stem pan (10 inch) that has been greased and dusted with flour. Bake at 300° for one hour and 40 minutes or until toothpick inserted in center comes out clean. Do not overbake. Allow cake to cool before removing from pan. This cake will keep for weeks.

Submitted by Adams Extract Co.

GERMAN CHOCOLATE POUND CAKE

2 cups sugar
1 cup shortening
4 eggs
2 tsps. "Adams Best" vanilla
2 tsps. Adams butter flavoring
1 cup buttermilk
3 cups all purpose flour, sifted
½ tsp. soda
1 tsp. salt
1 pkg. German sweet chocolate

Cream sugar and shortening. Add eggs. Add "Adams Best" vanilla, Adams butter flavoring and buttermilk. Sift together flour, soda and salt and add, mixing well. Then add German chocolate that has been softened in warm oven or in double boiler. Blend together well. Pour into a 9-inch stem pan or a 10-inch Bundt pan, which has been well greased and dusted with flour. Bake at 300° about 1½ hours or until toothpick inserted in center comes out clean. Remove cake from pan while still hot and place under a tight fitting cake cover and leave covered until cold.

Submitted by Adams Extract Co.

SOUP DE LA RIO GRANDE

6 medium white potatoes
4 large celery stalks
1 small onion
3 T. butter
Adkins "Texas Style" Fajita
  Seasoning

Peel and dice potatoes and place in enough water to cover well. Bring to a boil and let cook until tender. Dice onion and celery and saute in butter until they are of the desired firmness. Add to boiled potatoes. Add "Texas Style" fajita seasoning to taste.

Submitted by Adkins Seasoning Company

OAT NUT CEREAL
(contains natural rolled split oats and whole cot-n-nuts)

⅔ cup water   **½ cup Oat Nut cereal**

Stir Oat Nut into briskly boiling water. Reduce heat, cover and simmer for 1 minute. (Optional additions: salt, butter, honey or other natural sweeteners, or a whole egg.) Remove from heat and serve after 1 minute.

OTHER SUGGESTED USES FOR OAT NUT:
- Use in pancake or waffle mix. Just add an extra egg.
- Add Oat Nut to bran muffin mix or to cornbread muffin mix.
- Use a cup in meat loaf, salmon or tuna loaf.
- Make nutritious food out of a can of hominy, corn or English peas by adding some water and Oat Nut.
- Add Oat Nut to cookie dough mixtures.

Submitted by Aerobic Life Products

$5,000 FIESTA CHICKEN KIEV
(A Microwave BAKE OFF recipe)

4 whole chicken breasts, halved, boned and skinned
3 T. Butter
3 T. Old English style sharp cheese spread
2 tsps. instant minced onion
1 tsp. salt
1 tsp. monosodium glutamate
2 T. chopped green chiles

¼ cup melted butter
1 cup crushed cheddar cheese crackers
1½ T. taco seasoning mix
Shredded lettuce
Diced tomatoes
Chopped ripe olives
Chopped peanuts

Pound each side raw chicken with mallet or foil covered brick to flatten. Beat together butter and cheese spread until well blended. Mix in onion, salt, monosodium glutamate and chiles. Divide mixture evenly among the 8 flattened chicken pieces, placing a portion towards one end of each piece. Roll up each piece, tucking in ends to completely enclose filling. Fasten rolls with toothpicks. Dip each roll in melted butter to cover, then coat with mixture of cheese crackers and taco seasoning mix. Arrange rolls in 12 by 8 by 2 inch dish. Cover with wax paper. Place dish in microwave oven and cook 10 to 12 minutes. Serve chicken on a bed of shredded lettuce and diced tomatoes. Top with chopped olives and peanuts. If desired, serve with additional whole cloves, tomato wedges and your favorite taco sauce. Makes 8 servings.

Submitted by Aldus Marketing Association

4

ASPARAGUS CASSEROLE

2 cans (10½ oz.) asparagus,
  drained
1 can cheddar cheese soup
½ cup chopped roasted salted
  peanuts

¼ cup margarine
1 cup bread crumbs

Layer asparagus in a 2 quart casserole dish and pour soup over it. Sprinkle peanuts on top of asparagus mixture. Melt margarine and pour over bread crumbs. Top casserole with bread crumb mixture. Microwave 8 minutes on HIGH or until casserole is bubbly.

Submitted by Aldus Marketing Association

CRUSTY SWEET POTATO CASSEROLE

4 to 6 medium sweet potatoes,
  cooked
1 tsp. salt
¼ tsp. ground mace
1 egg, slightly beaten
⅓ cup crushed pineapple,
  drained

⅛ tsp. ground ginger
2 T. butter or margarine
1 T. orange juice
⅓ cup finely chopped, unsalted
  peanuts
⅓ cup flaked coconut
2 T. firmly packed brown sugar

Peel and mash sweet potatoes. Combine with salt, mace, egg, pineapple, ginger, butter and orange juice in a 1½ quart glass casserole. Microwave at HIGH for 5 to 6 minutes. Combine peanuts, coconut, and brown sugar. Sprinkle over casserole. Microwave at HIGH 3 to 4 minutes. Serve hot. Serves 6.

Submitted by Aldus Marketing Association

SWEET POTATO SOUFFLE

½ cup butter or margarine,
  divided
3 eggs, beaten
3 cups cooked, mashed sweet
  potatoes
1 cup sugar
1 cup milk

1 tsp. ground nutmeg
½ tsp. ground cinnamon
½ cup seedless raisins
¼ cup orange juice
1 cup corn flakes, crushed
½ cup chopped peanuts
½ cup firmly packed brown sugar

Place ¼ cup butter in a 2 quart casserole. Microwave at HIGH 30 seconds. Add eggs and sweet potato to butter. Stir to combine. Add sugar, milk, nutmeg, cinnamon, raisins and orange juice. Cover with wax paper. Microwave at HIGH for 15 to 16 minutes or until firm. Combine remaining butter and other ingredients in a bowl. Sprinkle over souffle. Microwave, uncovered, at HIGH for 2 minutes. Let stand, covered, 2 to 3 minutes before serving. Yields 6 to 8 servings.

Submitted by Aldus Marketing Association

5

HAM AND SWEET POTATO SURPRISE

1½ cups cubed ham
1 can (29 oz.) whole sweet
    potatoes, drained
1 T. butter or margarine

⅓ cup dark corn syrup
¼ cup crunchy peanut butter
¼ cup orange juice

Place ham in round glass baking dish. Slice sweet potatoes and arrange on top of ham. Place butter in a 1 quart glass bowl. Microwave on HIGH 30 seconds to melt. Stir in corn syrup, peanut butter, and orange juice. Pour over sweet potato and ham mixture. Microwave at HIGH for 4 minutes.

Submitted by Aldus Marketing Corporation

PEANUT CHICKEN CURRY

4 chicken breast halves, boned
    and skinned
¼ cup all purpose flour
4 T. butter or margarine
1 egg
⅓ cup crunchy peanut butter
1 tsp. curry powder
½ tsp. salt

⅛ tsp. black pepper
⅛ tsp. cayenne pepper
⅓ cup buttermilk
2 tsps. fresh lemon juice
½ cup seasoned dry bread
    crumbs
Chutney
Hot cooked rice

Wash and dry chicken pieces. Dip in flour. Set aside. Microwave butter in flat baking dish at HIGH for 30 seconds to melt. Set aside. Combine remaining ingredients except bread crumbs, chutney and rice. Mixture will be somewhat thick and should be well mixed. Dip floured chicken in peanut butter mixture, then in bread crumbs. Place chicken pieces in dish containing butter. Turn to coat well. Microwave, uncovered at HIGH 9 to 12 minutes. Rotate dish ½ turn after 5 to 6 minutes of microwaving. Cover with wax paper and let stand 2 to 3 minutes before serving. Serve with chutney and hot cooked rice. Yields 4 servings.

Variation: Instead of chutney substitute The Pepper Palate Sweet Pepper Relish.

Submitted by Aldus Marketing Corporation

CHICKEN PEANUT CASSEROLE

2 cups cooked chicken, diced
1 cup cooked rice
1 cup diced celery
½ cup plus 2 T. salted Spanish
    peanuts, roasted
½ cup salad dressing or
    mayonnaise
¼ tsp. salt

4 hard cooked eggs, sliced
2 tsp. dehydrated minced onion
2 T. lemon juice
1 can (10½ oz) cream of chicken
    soup, undiluted
¼ cup peanut butter
½ cup crumbled potato chips

Mix together chicken, eggs, rice, onion, celery, lemon juice, ½ cup peanuts, soup, salad dressing, peanut butter and salt. Turn into 1 ½ quart casserole suitable for use in microwave. Heat for 5 minutes on HIGH. Stir. Sprinkle with mixture of potato chip crumbs and 2 tablespoons peanuts. Return to microwave for 5 minutes. Makes 6 servings. (This casserole freezes well. Put it together and microwave for 5 minutes before freezing it.)

Submitted by Aldus Marketing Corporation

HOPPIN JOHN

2 T. vegetable oil
1 cup chopped cooked ham
1 cup finely chopped onions
½ tsp. hot pepper sauce

2 cans (15 oz. each) Allens or East Texas Fair fresh shelled blackeyed peas, undrained
3 cups cooked rice
½ tsp. salt

Heat oil in large skillet over medium high heat. Add ham, onions, and hot pepper sauce. Saute 3 to 5 minutes until onions are tender but not browned, stirring frequently. Add blackeyed peas, rice and salt. Reduce heat to medium low. Cover and cook 5 minutes until heated through.

OTHER USES FOR FRESH CANNED BLACKEYE PEAS:
• Add blackeye peas to chili.
• Add blackeyes to rice, okra and tomatoes.
• Add bacon drippings and onion to blackeyes for a side dish.
• Substitute blackeyed peas for potatoes as a side dish.

Submitted by Allen Canning Company

KATIE'S APPLE DUMPLINGS

2 cups flour
3/4 cup Crisco
¼ tsp. salt
⅓ cup milk
1 T. vinegar

4 medium size apples, peeled, cored and sliced thinly.
2 cups sugar, divided
Apple pie spice
4 tsps. margarine

Cut shortening into flour and salt. Add vinegar to milk and work into the dry mixture. Roll on floured board to about ⅛ inch thickness. Cut into four pieces, each about 5 inches square. Onto each pastry square, place ¼ of the apple slices, ¼ cup sugar, sprinkle with spice and 1 tsp. margarine. Fold corners over, enclosing filling. Repeat until all squares are filled. Place dumplings in a 10 by 10 by 3 inch baking dish. Pour 1 cup sugar over all. Place 1 tsp. margarine on top of each dump-ling. Pour very hot water in dish to fill within 1 inch of top. Let stand 5 minutes. Bake 45 minutes or until brown, in a 375° oven.

Submitted by Ambrosia Orchards

SEVEN LAYER DIP

In a shallow dish, approximately 14 by 18 inches, layer the following ingredients:

2 cans (10½ oz) Amigos Bean Dip Guacamole (purchase guacamole dip in the refrigerated section of your store, or make your own by mashing 2 ripe avocados and adding 1 tsp. lemon juice, ½ tsp. salt and ⅛ tsp garlic powder.)

8 oz. sour cream	**1 medium tomato, chopped**
1 can (10½ oz) Amigos Picante	**1 cup cheddar cheese, grated**
Sauce	**1 small can black olives, chopped**

Serve immediately or refrigerate until serving time. Serve with tostados or nacho chips or large Fritos. Serves 8 to 12 persons as a party dip.

EDITOR'S NOTE: Refried beans may be substitued for the bean dip. Amigos also puts up cans of refried beans, as well as enchilada sauce and taco sauce.

Submitted by Amigos Canning Co.

SWEET PEPPER RELISH COLE SLAW

1 medium head cabbage,	**1 tsp. sugar**
shredded	**1 small garlic clove, pressed**
¼ cup chopped onion	**¼ cup shredded celery or ½ tsp.**
1 small carrot, shredded	**celery seed (optional)**
½ cup mayonnaise	**2 T. The PEPPER PALATE Sweet**
1 oz. cider vinegar	**Pepper Relish (red)**
¼ tsp. salt	

Mix and serve. Best served after chilling.

Submitted by Linda Jordan for Angel Craft Inc.

PEPPER RELISH SURPRISE CORN MUFFINS

1 cup enriched cornmeal	**1 cup milk**
1 cup all purpose flour	**1 egg**
¼ cup sugar	**¼ cup vegetable oil**
4 tsp. baking powder	**½ cup PEPPER PALATE Sweet**
½ tsp. salt	**Pepper Relish**

In medium bowl, combine cornmeal, flour, sugar, baking powder and salt. Combine milk, egg and oil. Add to dry ingredients, mixing just until dry ingredients are moistened. Fill greased, medium-size muffin cups ⅔ full of cornmeal mixture. Place 1½ teaspoons relish in center of each muffin cup; press lightly into batter. Bake at 425° for 15 to 20 minutes. Cool 5 minutes in muffin pans, remove to wire cooling rack. Makes 12 muffins.

NOTE: The Sweet Pepper Relish from THE PEPPER PALATE is available in three colors — red, green and gold — and in two taste levels — hot or mild — in each color. Any of these six varieties may be used in the above recipe for variation in color and piquancy.

Submitted by Angel Craft Inc.

SWEET PEPPER RELISH MOLD

1 carton of whipped Philadelphia cream cheese
1 round tsp. horseradish
1 small can clams, minced and drained

Several dashes of Beau Monde seasoning salt
2 to 3 T. finely minced onion
1 jar The PEPPER PALATE Sweet Pepper Relish (red, hot)

Let carton of cheese sit at room temperature for 30 minutes. Then stir in all seasonings (except for relish) and place in refrigerator to harden in its own carton mold. Unmold when ready to serve onto dish with inclined or low sides. Pour relish over mold. Serve with Melba toast.

Submitted by Angel Craft Inc.

RING AROUND THE BAGEL

Toast or warm bagel. Spread with cream cheese. Top with The PEPPER PALATE Sweet Pepper Relish in a ring around the bagel.

NOTE: Pepper relish comes in three colors — red, green and gold — and in two taste levels — hot or mild. Any of them work in the above recipe, depending on your taste buds.

Submitted by Lewis Nesman for Angel Craft Inc.

SALLY'S SUPREME SURPRISE

For each serving:

1 half chicken breast, skinned, boned, flatted slightly
1 piece Monterey Jack cheese
1 T. The Pepper Palate Sweet Pepper Relish

Bread crumbs
Parmesan cheese
White wine

Lay cheese and relish on breast and fold over. Secure with tooth-pick. Sprinkle each breast with bread crumbs and Parmesan cheese. Place in casserole. Pour a little white wine in dish. Bake at 350° for 40 minutes.

Submitted by Sally Nesman for Angel Craft

SESAME PEPPER CHEESE LOG

1 pkg. (3 oz.) cream cheese
¼ cup rose wine
3 T. The PEPPER PALATE Sweet Pepper Relish
¼ tsp. salt
¾ lb. Jack cheese, grated
⅓ cup toasted sesame seeds

Beat cream cheese until soft. Blend in wine, pepper relish, salt and Jack cheese. Shape into a log 2 inches in diameter and about 10 inches long. Toast sesame seeds in 400° oven until golden, about 5 minutes. Roll cheese log in sesame seeds. Chill until firm, about 2 hours. Makes 1 pound log.

Submitted by Angel Craft Inc.

PEARS CARDINAL

6 fresh pears
2 cups water
1½ cups sugar
¼ tsp. salt
1 T. lemon juice
1 jar (8 oz.) The PEPPER PALATE Sweet Pepper Relish (red)
½ cup The PEPPER PALATE Mild Pepper Jelly (red)

Peel pears, leaving stems on. Mix water, sugar, lemon juice and salt in a saucepan. Bring to a boil. Add whole pears. Simmer, turning pears occasionally in syrup for 20 to 25 minutes or until tender. Cool pears in syrup. Remove pears. Combine relish and jelly in top of double boiler. Melt over low heat. Remove from heat and chill. To serve, place pears upright either individually or together in flat dish. Spoon sauce over pears.

Submitted by Angel Craft Inc.

THERESA'S POTATO SALAD

3 lbs. potatoes, cooked and sliced
4 hardboiled eggs, chopped
3 stalks celery, chopped
1 medium onion, chopped
3 T. The PEPPER PALATE Sweet Pepper Relish (red, hot)
1 T. sweet pickle relish (opt.)
2 cups Hellman's mayonnaise
2 T. yellow mustard
½ cup sour cream or plain yogurt (opt.)
¼ tsp. dill weed
1 tsp. garlic powder
1 tsp. low salt seasoning
Paprika

Combine all vegetables in a large bowl. In separate bowl, combine all other ingredients except paprika. Pour over vegetables and toss thoroughly but gently. Sprinkle top generously with paprika. Chill at least 2 hours before serving.

Submitted by Teresa Fay for Angel Craft Inc.

THERESA'S MACARONI SALAD

1 pkg. (1 lb.) elbow macaroni,
   cooked as directed, drained
3 stalks celery, chopped
1 medium onion, chopped
3 T. The PEPPER PALATE Sweet
   Pepper Relish (green or red,
   hot)

2 cups Hellman's mayonnaise
2 T. yellow mustard
¼ tsp. dill weed
1 tsp. garlic powder
1 tsp. low salt seasoning
2 boiled eggs, sliced
Paprika

Combine first three ingredients in large bowl. Set aside. Combine remaining ingredients except for eggs and paprika. Mix well. Pour over mixture in first bowl. Toss lightly. Garnish with sliced eggs. Sprinkle generously with paprika. Chill at least 2 hours before serving.

NOTE: Dressing makes an excellent vegetable dip for cauliflower, asparagus, broccoli, squash, etc.

Submitted by Theresa Fay for Angel Craft Inc.

POLISH PICKLED PEPPER BEANS

For this recipe, any style of bean may be used: Whole green beans, fresh or frozen, cooked and drained; French style green beans, fresh or frozen, cooked and drained; Yellow wax beans, fresh or canned, cooked and drained; Romano (Italian) green beans, fresh or frozen, cooked and drained; English peas, fresh or frozen, cooked and drained; Blackeyed peas, canned, dry or fresh, cooked and drained; Kidney beans, canned or dry, cooked and drained; Pinto beans, canned or dry, cooked and drained; Garbanzo beans, canned or dry, cooked and drained; or a combination of any of the above.

Drain 1 jar The PEPPER PALATE Polish Pickled Peppers. Reserve juice and use to marinate beans for several hours or overnight in refrigerator.Turn beans into bowl and garnish with the red pepper strips of Polish Pickled Peppers.

Submitted by Angel Craft Inc.

TEXAS CITRUS PUNCH

3 cups fresh orange juice, chilled
2 cups fresh grapefruit juice,
   chilled
1 cup fresh lemon juice, chilled

½ to ¾ cup sugar
1 cup Artesia Sparkling Mineral
   Water

Garnishes: strawberries, pineapple spears, orange slices or wedges, lemon or lime slices, cherries, whatever is in season.

Combine fruit juices and sugar. Stir until dissolved. Pour over ice, add mineral water. Garnish punch with fruit on skewers or on individual glasses.

Submitted by Editor for Artesia Waters Inc.

REFRIED BEANS

½ lb. dry beans, cooked
⅓ cup melted lard or ham fat or
   pork drippings or bacon
   drippings

¼ cup onion, finely chopped
Bellville Stoneground Corn
   Tortilla Chips

Heat the fat in a skillet and fry the onions without letting them brown, until they are soft. Add 1 cup of beans and mash them until you have a coarse puree. Add the remaining beans a little at a time, continuing mashing. Add some of the bean broth as you go. Let the puree cook over a fairly high heat until it begins to dry out and sizzle. It should come away from the surface of the pan. Continue cooking for 15 to 20 minutes, tipping the pan from side to side and forcing the bean mixture into the center of the pan. It will form a roll which you can then tip out of the pan onto a serving dish. Into the roll, stick several tortilla chips. Serve with additional tortilla chips for dipping. tortilla chips may also be used to dip guacamole or with a Mexican Layered Salad or with picante sauce.

Submitted by Editor for Bellville Tortilla Chip

OLD COWTOWN CHILI PIE

1 pkg. Ben's Old Cowtown Chili
   Mix

3 lbs. ground or chili meat.

Prepare as directed on package. Put on simmer. Using individual bowls, add any or all of the following: Fritos, diced tomatoes, green onions, shredded cheese. Then spoon Ben's Old Cowntown Chili over your ingredients and enjoy.

Submitted by Ben's Specialty Food and Spices

OLD COWTOWN B.B.Q.

Select your favorite meat—chicken, beef, pork, hamburgers. Roll in Ben's Old Cowtown B.B.Q. Dust and put it on the grill. Simple as that.

Submitted by Ben's Specialty Foods and Spices

CHICKEN BREASTS PIQUANT

3 whole chicken breasts
1 T. salad oil
1 tsp. dried leaf tarragon
½ cup BIG TEX grapefruit juice

1 tsp. salt
⅛ tsp. pepper
¾ tsp. paprika

Place halved breasts, skin side down, in shallow, foil lined baking dish. Combine remaining ingredients. Brush over chicken. Bake in 375° oven for 45 to 50 minutes, turning after first 25 minutes and brushing occasionally with sauce. Yield: 6 servings, 145 calories per serving.

Submitted by BigTex, Texas Citrus Exchange

HONEY BRAN MUFFINS

1 cup all bran cereal
1 cup enriched flour
2½ tsp. baking powder
½ tsp. salt
¾ cup buttermilk

1 egg slightly beaten
¼ cup shortening, melted
¼ cup honey
Honey

Combine all dry ingredients in a mixing bowl. Make a well in center. Combine milk, egg, shortening and ¼ cup honey. Add all at once to dry ingredients and stir only until dry ingredients are moistened. Fill muffin pans ⅔ full. Top batter in each muffin pan with 1 teaspoon honey. Bake at 375° for about 20 minutes. Makes 12 small or 8 large muffins.

Submitted by Blackland Apiaries

SUGGESTED USES FOR TEXAS HONEY

• Honey Butter — Whip ½ cup softened butter and slowly add ½ cup honey. Add some grated orange rind if desired.
• Fruit Salad Dressing — Mix equal parts fresh lime juice and honey. Add a pinch of powdered ginger and pour over a fruit salad.
• Honeyed Grapefruit — Drizzle honey over the top of a sectioned grapefruit half. Heat under the broiler for 3 to 5 minutes. Don't let it burn!
• Quick Pick Up — Mix in a blender 1 cup orange juice, 1 T. honey, 1 raw egg and some ice cubes. Great in the morning!
• Meat Glaze — Combine ½ cup honey, ¼ cup soy sauce, and 1 tsp. mustard for a glaze for meats or ham.
• Honey Balls — Mix equal parts honey, peanut butter, dry milk, graham cracker crumbs, and raisins or chopped peanuts. Shape into 1 inch balls and roll in coconut or dip in chocolate.
• Add a couple of tablespoons of honey to your favorite cake or muffin mix for added flavor and moistness.

Submitted by Blackland Apiaries

FRESH BLUEBERRY PIE

One baked pie crust (9 inch)
¼ cup cold water
5 T. all purpose flour
Pinch of salt

4 cups fresh blueberries
1 cup sugar
½ cup water
Whipped cream or topping

Using the ¼ cup water, make a smooth paste with flour and salt. Boil 1 cup blueberries with sugar and ½ cup water. Add flour mixture and stir until thick. Cool and add remaining blueberries. Put mixture in pie shell and refrigerate. When cold, top with whipped cream.

Submitted by The Blueberry Patch

BOLNER'S FAMILY DELUXE CHILI

1 T. oil
2 lbs. chili meat
4 cloves garlic
15 oz. can tomato sauce
1 quart chicken broth
5 T. oil
4 T. flour

4 T. Fiesta "No Salt" Fancy Light
   Chili Powder
½ tsp. Fiesta whole comino
½ tsp. Fiesta ground black pepper
½ tsp. MSG
½ tsp. salt (optional)

Peel and chop the garlic. SLOWLY brown the meat and the garlic in 1 tablespoon oil. Add the tomato sauce, the chicken broth, MSG and salt. SIMMER one hour. Heat the 5 tablespoons of oil in a sauce pan over medium low heat. Fry the flour, pepper, comino and the chili powder for 5 minutes. Add this roux to the meat. SIMMER over low heat for ½ hour. Serve in bowls with hot tortillas. Chili is always better the next day.

NOTE: For QUICK delicious chili, use Bolner's Fiesta Brand Quick Chili Mix.

Submitted by Bolner's Fiesta Products

CHILI

2 lbs. lean coarse ground meat
   (beef and/or pork)
2 cloves fresh garlic, chopped
1 onion, chopped
2 T. Fiesta chili pepper
¼ tsp. Fiesta whole comino

¼ tsp. Fiesta whole Mexican
   oregano
1 can (15 oz.) tomato sauce
1 quart beef broth
1 T. oil
Salt to taste

Brown the meat in the oil. Add the onion, garlic and comino and continue browning until onions are clear. Add the broth, tomato and salt. Bring to a boil and SIMMER for 1 hour. Add the chili pepper and the oregano and SIMMER for 1 more hour until done.

Submitted by Bolner's Fiesta Products

PANHANDLE FAVORITE BRISKET

3 lbs. B3R Beef brisket
3 T. liquid smoke
2½ tsp. garlic salt

1½ tsp. onion salt
1½ tsp celery salt

Mix ingredients and marinate brisket overnight in a baking bag. Next morning, add: 3 T. Worcestershire sauce, black pepper to taste. Cook in a 250° oven for 6 hours. For larger brisket, add ingredients in like proportions to weight of meat.

Submitted by Bradley 3 Ranch, B3R Country Meats

BRAZOS VALLEY PEACH ICE CREAM
(1985 Freeze-Off Grand Prize Winner)

2 cans (14 oz.) CONDENSED (not evaporated) milk
2 milk cans of water
2 pkgs. (3 oz.) peach gelatin
1 small pinch of salt
6 eggs well beaten
2 pints of whipping cream

2 T. vanilla extract
1 T. almond extract
2 T. lemon juice
4 cups chopped, fresh peaches
Few drops yellow food coloring (optional)

Combine CONDENSED milk with 1 can of water in top of double boiler. Boil the other can of water and dissolve the gelatin in this. Add this to mixture in double boiler. (This will curdle slightly). Heat over simmering water for 10 minutes, stirring occasionally. When hot, beat smooth and remove from heat. In large bowl, beat eggs well. Gradually add hot mixture to eggs, mixing constantly. In a bowl, crush peaches with mixer—or in a food processor or blender—until there are no large pieces. Add the peaches and all remaining ingredients to mixture in large bowl and mix well. Chill for several hours or preferably overnight. This will be like very soft custard after chilling. Pour into freezer can and freeze. Allow to ripen at least 2 hours. (If needed, add milk to fill freezer can to proper level.)

VARIATION: This recipe could be used with raspberries, blackberries or strawberries with those flavors of gelatin.

Submitted by Brazos Valley Orchards

RIBBONCANE PECAN PIE

1 cup sugar
2 T. flour
1 T. butter
1 cup ribboncane syrup
1 tsp. vanilla

3 eggs
¼ tsp. salt
1 cup pecan pieces
1 unbaked 9 inch pie shell

Place pecans in pie shell. Blend all of the remaining ingredients in blender container or with mixer. Pour over pecans in pie shell. Bake at 425° for 10 minutes, then at 350° for 50 minutes or until set.

Submitted by Brockett-Tyree Farms

TEXAS PEANUT BRITTLE

Boil until a thread forms: **1 cup sugar, ½ cup hot water, and ½ cup syrup — either ribboncane or sorghum**
Add: **1 cup peanuts (raw)**
Cook until a light brown color. Remove from heat. Stir in: **1 tsp. soda, 1 tsp. vanilla, and 1 tsp. butter**
Pour out on greased cookie sheet to cool.

Submitted by Brockett-Tyree Farms

SORGHUM BRAN MUFFINS

1 cup all bran cereal
½ cup milk
½ cup sorghum syrup
1 egg
¼ cup shortening

½ cup raisins
1 cup flour
2½ tsp. baking powder
½ tsp. salt

Combine first three ingredients. Let stand until liquid is absorbed. Add remaining ingredients. Stir until just combined. Fill greased muffin cups ⅔ full. Bake at 400° for 20 minutes. Makes 12 muffins.

Submitted by Brockett-Tyree Farms

SUSIE'S DEVIL'S FOOD CAKE
(1986 State Fair Grand Prize Winner)

2 cups sugar   1 cup Crisco

Cream well and add:

3 eggs, 1 at a time

Beat well after each addition and add:

1 cup buttermilk   1 tsp. salt
1 tsp. vanilla

Beat well. Mix together in separate bowl:

½ cup cocoa   2 tsps. soda
2½ cups Light Crust All Purpose
    Flour, unsifted

Add alternately to mixture with 1 cup boiling water, mixing well after each addition. Pour batter evenly into 3 greased and floured 9 inch cake pans. Bake in 350° oven about 30 minutes. When top of cake springs back upon touching, the cake is done. Cool in pans 10 minutes and on racks 30 minutes before frosting.

ICING:

1 cup sugar   4 T. water
Dash cream of tartar   ½ cup light corn syrup

Boil above mixture slowly until it spins a thread 6 to 8 inches long or until candy thermometer reaches 230°. Meanwhile beat until stiff:

3 egg whites   1½ tsps. vanilla
Dash cream of tartar

Pour syrup into egg whites while mixer is running on high speed. Beat until it holds its shape or stands in peaks. Garnish with chocolate if desired. (This recipe may be doubled.)

Submitted by Cargill Flour Milling (Burrus Light Crust)

16

WICK FOWLER'S HOT CHEESE DIP

2 lbs. Velveeta cheese
1 can cream of mushroom soup
1 lb. ground beef

1 lb. sausage — mild
1 jar (12 oz.) of Wick Fowler's
    Picante Sauce

In a crockpot, melt cheese. In a skillet, cook ground beef and sausage until brown. Add meats, soup and picante sauce to cheese. Stir well. Serve in crock pot or transfer to chafing dish. Keep warm. Serves approximately 25 to 30. Excellent with tostados, Fritos or party crackers.

Submitted by Caliente Chili Inc.

RANCHO CASSEROLE 2-ALARM STYLE

1 pkg. (3⅝ oz.) Wick Fowler's 2-
    Alarm Chili Ingredients
1 can (8 oz.) tomato sauce
2 lbs. chili ground beef

1 can (20 oz.) pinto or kidney
    beans (optional)
½ cup chopped onions
1½ cups grated cheese
1 pkg. (6 oz.) cornbread mix

Prepare chili, using instructions on package. Stir in beans, pour into 2-quart casserole. Sprinkle onions and cheese over chili. Prepare cornbread according to package directions (jalapeno cornbread mix, optional). Spoon prepared cornbread mix (still wet) over mixture. Bake in 400° oven for 20 to 25 minutes or until cornbread browns. Serve with salad and beverage. Serves 6 to 8.

Submitted by Caliente Chili Inc.

WICK FOWLER'S LENTIL SOUP

1 lb. dried lentils
8 cups cold water
2 stalks celery, chopped
1 medium onion, chopped
2 carrots, sliced in rounds
1 clove fresh garlic, minced

1 can (16 oz.) tomatoes, diced
½ cup diced ham
1 pkg. (1¼ oz.) Wick Fowler's
    Bean Seasoning
2 tsps. salt or salt substitute

Put all ingredients with water into a medium size sauce pan. Bring to a boil. Reduce heat and cover. Simmer 45 minutes to an hour or until beans are tender. Stir occasionally and add water if necessary.

Submitted by Caliente Chili Inc.

WICK FOWLER'S BARBECUED CHICKEN

8 chicken thighs
1 pkg. (12 oz.) Wick Fowler's
    Barbecue Sauce Kit

1 T. Worcesterchire sauce
Juice of ½ lemon
Fresh minced parsley for garnish

Skin chicken thighs, if desired. Place in an oven proof dish. Combine barbecue sauce (prepared), Worcestershire sauce, and lemon juice.

Pour over chicken and bake at 325° for 45 minutes or until done. Sprinkle with parsley. Serves 4.

Submitted by Caliente Chili Inc.

WICK FOWLER'S BEEFED-UP BLACK-EYED PEA SOUP

2 lbs. ground beef
¼ cup minced green pepper
1 cup cream of chicken soup, undiluted
2 cans (14 oz. ea.) chicken broth
1 quart water
1 pkg. Wick Fowler's Bean Seasoning

1 can (28 oz.) whole tomatoes, undrained
1 pkg. (16 oz.) frozen black-eyed peas
1 small onion, chopped
1 cup chopped celery
½ tsp. salt or more to taste

Brown beef with green pepper. Then drain. In a large soup pot pour in beef mixture and remainder of ingredients. Bring to a boil and cover. Simmer for about 1 hour. Yields 4½ quarts. Serve with cornbread, crackers or chunks of French bread. NOTE: Pinto beans or black beans may be substituted for peas.

Submitted by Caliente Chili Inc.

WICK FOWLER'S CHICKEN ENCHILADAS SUISSAS

12 corn tortillas
  Cooking oil
½ cup chopped onion
2 T. butter
4 cups cooked chicken, cut in bite size pieces
1 cup sour cream

1 can cream of chicken soup
1 pkg (1¼ oz.) Wick Fowler's Taco Seasoning
1 can cream of mushroom soup
1 (4 oz.) can chopped green chiles
1 cup grated Swiss cheese

Fry tortillas quickly in oil to soften. Drain. Saute onion in butter. Heat remaining ingredients except for cheese. Add to onion mixture. Fill each tortilla with a spoonful of chicken mixture. Roll and put in a lightly greased 9 by 13 inch baking dish, seam side down. Pour remaining mixture over tortillas and top with Swiss cheese. Bake at 350° about 30 minutes or until bubbly. Serves 4 to 6.

Submitted by Caliente Chili

GRILLED CHILI CHICKEN 2-ALARM STYLE

1 pkg. (3⅝ oz.) Wick Fowler's 2-Alarm Chili Ingredients
2 cups dried bread crumbs

¼ cup vegetable or corn oil
1 broiler or fryer, about 2½ lbs., skinned and cut up

Combine 2-Alarm Chili Ingredients (omit the masa flour and add red pepper only if you like it hot) in large plastic bag with bread crumbs. Place 1 cup of the crumb mixture in a medium plastic bag. Brush oil on all sides of chicken in foil lined jelly roll pan. Add chicken pieces, a few at a time, into the medium bag. Close and shake, coating pieces evenly. Bake in oven at 375° for 45 minutes or until fork tender. To grill, place pieces on lightly oiled sheet of heavy duty aluminum foil over grill. Grill about 6 inches above medium low coals about 30 minutes or until fork tender. Store leftover crumbs in a jar. Will keep for a month.

Submitted by Caliente Chili Inc.

BRAISED BEEF IN CHILI WINE SAUCE 2-ALARM STYLE

1 pkg. (3⅝ oz.) Wick Fowler's 2-Alarm Chili Ingredients
4 lbs. beef stew meat, cut in 1¼ inch cubes
1 jar or can (5¼ oz.) condensed beef broth, undiluted
1 bottle (fifth) red Burgundy wine
2 bay leaves
1 tsp. thyme leaves
1½ lbs. small white boiling onions
1 lb. small mushrooms, halved
¼ cup butter or margarine, softened
⅓ cup all purpose flour
2 T. chopped parsley

In 8 quart sauce pot, add ¼ of the stew meat. Cook until lightly browned, removing pieces to bowl as they brown. When all beef is browned, pour off any remaining fat from pot. Return beef to pot. Add broth, wine, bay leaves and thyme. Heat to boiling, cover and cook over low heat 1 hour. Add all packets of chili ingredients except salt, red pepper and masa. Add onions and mushrooms. Cover and cook 30 minutes or until beef and onions are tender. Meanwhile in small bowl, blend or mix butter with flour and masa until smooth. Stir a small amount of hot beef liquid into flour mixture until flowable. Stir flour mixture into beef and cook until thickened. Discard bay leaves. Taste for seasoning and add salt and pepper if desired. Spoon into large serving bowl or chafing dish. Sprinkle with parsley. Serve with rice. Makes 8 to 10 servings.

Submitted by Caliente Chili Inc.

WURST PATE IN TEXAS

½ lb. Carlton's fully cooked smoked beef sausage, finely minced (in food processor or by hand)
8 oz. cream cheese, softened
2 tsp. minced onion, drained
1 tsp. fresh parsley, minced
½ tsp. Louisiana hot sauce (or hot sauce of your choice)
Rye Krisp crackers or toast points

Combine sausage, cheese, onions, parsley and hot sauce. Blend well. FOR HOT HORS D'OEUVRES: Spread over Rye Krisp crackers or toast points liberally, making sure to cover all area of crackers or toast to prevent burning. Place under broiler until puffy and light golden brown, about 2 minutes. Watch closely. Serve immediately. FOR COLD HORS D'OEUVRES: Mound in pretty bowl as for spread or fill celery ribs, jalapeno peppers, raw mushrooms, cherry tomatoes, etc.

EDITOR's NOTE: This recipe was the winner of the best hors d'oeuvre category.

Submitted by Mrs. Cherry C. Queen for Carlton's

CARLTON'S SAUSAGE SALAD

1½ lb. Carlton's beef sausage,
casing removed, sliced thinly
¼ cup red wine vinegar
2 tsps. prepared Dijon mustard
½ cup cooking oil
½ cup broken walnut meats

2 cups sliced celery
1 clove garlic, crushed
2 cups seeded, chopped tomatoes
1 cup sliced, blanched green
beans
1 cup cubed Mozzarella cheese
¼ cup chopped fresh basil leaves

In large skillet, brown sausage until crispy. Drain on paper towel. Clean skillet. In large bowl, combine vinegar and mustard. Set aside. Heat oil over medium heat in a large skillet. Add walnuts and saute until they begin to brown. Toss in celery and garlic. Cook, stirring constantly, until celery begins to soften, about 2 to 3 minutes. Remove pan from heat. Mix in remaining ingredients. Blend in vinegar-mustard mixture. Toss gently. Serve immediately on large flat greens, such as Boston or leaf lettuce. Serves 4.

EDITOR'S NOTE: This recipe was a grand prize winner.

Submitted by Ms. Beatrice Ortiz for Carlton's

JENNY'S TEX-MEX GERMAN SAUSAGE SUPPER PIE

3 eggs
2 T. oil
2 T. water
2 cups all purpose flour (do not
pre-sift)
1 tsp. double acting baking
powder
½ tsp. salt
1 T. oil

¾ lb. Carlton's Smoked Sausage
Links
3 eggs
3 cups small curd cottage cheese
½ cup chopped green onions
2 cans (4 oz. each) diced green
chilies
6 hard cooked eggs, shelled
1 egg yolk
1 T. water

In a small bowl, beat eggs, oil and water. Sift flour, baking powder and salt into a medium size mixing bowl. Make a well in center and pour in egg mixture. Stir with fork until blended. Turn dough onto lightly floured pastry board. Cover dough with the mixing bowl and let rest about 20 minutes. Make the filling while dough rests. After dough has rested, knead until smooth, about 3 minutes. Now, grease a 10 inch pie plate. Divide pastry and roll out half into a 13 inch circle and fit into pie plate. Trim edges and reserve trimmings. If filling has not been completed, refrigerate pie and trimmings. Saute sausage links in 1 T. oil until browned on all sides. Drain off fat. Slice sausage links into ¼ inch slices. Beat eggs thoroughly, add cheese, green onions, chilies and sausage slices. Pour ¾ of filling into pastry lined pie plate. Make 6 indentations in filling with the back of a wooden spoon and place one egg in each indentation. Cover with remaining filling. Roll out remaining pastry into a 12 inch circle and cut into 8 to 10 small stars. Place pastry on top of filling and fold edges of top crust under the bottom crust. Press together to seal. Crimp edges. Take a Texas cookie cutter and cut out this shape in the top crust, but do not remove. (This will be the escape slits for the steam.) Now, place the stars around the outside edges of the pie. Brush top with the egg yolk beaten with 1 T. water. Bake 35 to 40 minutes in a 400° oven. Serve warm or cold. Makes 8 generous servings.

EDITOR'S NOTE: This recipe was a winner of the best entree category.

Submitted by Mrs. Jeanette Felger for Carlton's

A NEW KIND OF DIPPER

Carlton summer sausage or Carlton smoked sausage

Slice either Carlton's summer sausage or Carlton's regular smoked sausage into very thin slices. Working with about 10 slices of summer sausage or 35 slices of regular sausage, place sausage in a ring (small ones in a double ring) on a microwave bacon rack or disposable dish. Put a white paper towel under the sausage slices and another white paper towel over the slices. Microwave for 3 to 4 minutes (depending on how thin the slices are) until the slices are well done. Let stand for a few minutes to crisp up. Use as dippers with your favorite dip or spread.

Submitted by Priscilla Hanz for Carlton's

MARINATED SALAD

1 fresh bunch broccoli, cut into bite size pieces
1 head of cauliflower, cut into bite size pieces
2 links of Carlton's beef sausage, chopped or sliced
1 can of black olives, sliced
1 jar of green olives, whole
1 cup cherry tomatoes

1 jar marinated artichokes, quartered
1 cup celery, chopped
2 bunches green onions, chopped
1 jar (8 oz.) Zesta Italian dressing
2 carrots, sliced thin
8 oz. fresh mushrooms, quartered, if small leave whole

Marinate all in the Italian dressing for at least one day before serving. The tomatoes are best if added just before serving.

Submitted by Marge Clyde for Carlton's

SAUSAGE AND BLACKEYED PEAS

1 lb. Carlton's sausage, sliced
1 pkg. frozen blackeyes (fresh may be substituted)
1 small onion, chopped

1 green pepper, chopped
3 T. Lea & Perrins
1 tsp. garlic powder
salt and pepper as desired.

Place peas, onion, green pepper, Lea & Perrins, garlic powder and salt and pepper if desired in pan and cover with water. Bring to a boil, cover tightly and cook on medium low until peas are tender, about 1 hour. Check occasionally to see if more liquid is needed. When peas are tender, add sliced sausage and cook on low for 20 minutes. Serves 2.

Submitted by Donna Francis for Carlton's Sausage

BLACK BEANS WITH SAUSAGE AND RUM

1 lb. dry black beans
2 bay leaves
1 medium onion, chopped
2 T. oil
½ lb. Carlton's smoked sausage, sliced
1 can (10½ oz.) consomme, undiluted

1 clove garlic, crushed or ¼ tsp. garlic powder
½ tsp. oregano
1 tsp. salt
½ cup rum (optional)

Soak beans in water to cover for 8 hours or overnight. Cook until tender with bay leaves. Drain and remove bay leaves. Saute onion in oil until transparent in a 3 quart pan. Add sausage, consomme, garlic, oregano, salt, rum and drained beans. Simmer 1 hour. (Add water if needed, or bean juice.) Serves 4.

Submitted by Priscilla Hanz for Carlton's Sausage

SAUSAGE TIDBITS

1 jar (12 oz.) Del Monte chili sauce
1½ lb. Carlton's wurst

1 cup grape jelly

In electric skillet or chafing dish, mix chili sauce and grape jelly. Heat until jelly is melted and sauce is simmering. Cut wurst into bite size circles, about ¼ inch thick. Add to sauce. Simmer on low heat. Serve with cocktail toothpicks. NOTE: This can also be served as an entree. Just cut the sausage into larger serving sized pieces.

Submitted by Jill Rathburn for Carlton's

SWEET & SOUR SAUSAGE

2 lbs. Carlton's sausage, sliced into 1 inch pieces

2 jars (10 oz. each) red currant jelly
1 jar (10 oz.) of mustard

Empty jelly in sauce pan. Fill one of the empty jelly jars with mustard. Empty mustard into pan. (Always use twice as much jelly as mustard.) Heat jelly and mustard until melted and mixed well. Add sausage and heat mixture until slightly simmering. Serve warm. May be prepared ahead of time and reheated.

Submitted by Donna Francis for Carlton's

BERRY STEEPED CHOCOLATE CAKE

6¼ oz. semisweet chocolate
1¼ oz. unsweetened chocolate
15 T. butter
1 jar (11½ oz.) seedless rasperry
  or blackberry jam

1 T. orange liquer
5 eggs, separated
⅞ cup superfine sugar
½ cup cake flour

RICH CHOCOLATE GLAZE (recipe follows)

Heat oven to 350°. Butter and flour a 9 by 13 inch baking pan or line it with parchment paper. Melt chocolates in a double boiler over hot water. Add butter and stir until smooth. Remove from heat. Add liquer to jam and stir well. Set aside. Beat egg yolks with half the superfine sugar until mixture is light in color and forms a ribbon when trailed from beater. Stir the chocolate mixture into the yolks. Add the jam mixture into the chocolate/egg yolk mixture. Beat egg whites until frothy. Add the remaining sugar and beat to soft peak stage. Sift cake flour and fold into chocolate mixture. Fold in whites gently. Spread batter in prepared pan and smooth top with spatula. Bake in preheated oven until a toothpick inserted in middle comes out clean, about 25 minutes. Cool. Put a baking sheet on top of cooled cake and flip cake over onto sheet. Cover with plastic wrap and chill. Meanwhile make glaze.

GLAZE:

½ lb. semisweet chocolate   ½ lb. butter

Melt chocolate in double boiler over hot water. Stir in butter, one tablespoon at a time. Each piece should partially melt before the next is added. If mixture starts to thin out after you have added about half the butter, remove it from the heat and continue adding the rest of the butter. Make sure the butter is thoroughly incorporated and leaves no streaks. Glaze should be thick enough to set rather quickly, but if it is too thick, it will be difficult to spread a thin layer. To test consistency, hold some of the glaze above the pan and let it drip back in. It should be visible for 2 to 4 seconds, before disappearing into the rest of the glaze. To adjust, let cool to thicken and heat gently to thin.

Submitted by Catlett Creek Berry Farm

BUFFALO ROAST IN BROWN BAG

3 to 4 lbs. buffalo roast   Seasonings as desired

Place meat in shallow roasting pan. Add seasonings. Slide pan and meat into a large brown paper bag. Secure end by folding over and fastening with paper clips. Bake in 350° oven until internal temperature reaches 170° or approximately 2½ to 3 hours. Do not overcook. Makes 6 to 8 servings.

Submitted by Cedar Mountain Ranch

BUFFALO ROAST IN FOIL

3 to 4 lb. buffalo roast   ½ envelope dry onion soup

Preheat oven to 425°. Place roast on an ample piece of heavy duty aluminum foil. Sprinkle ½ envelope of dry onion soup mix over the mix. Bring edges of foil together and seal tightly using a "drugstore wrap." Place in shallow roasting pan and bake 1½ to 2 hours. Ample juices collect within the foil; this may be thickened for gravy. Makes 6 servings.

Drugstore Wrap: Bring edges of foil together, fold over to ¾ inch, continue to fold down to make a tight wrap around the meat. Ends of foil may be folded up and over in a similar manner.

Submitted by Cedar Mountain Ranch

BUFFALO ROAST IN PLASTIC BAKING BAG

3 to 4 lb. buffalo roast	1 bay leaf
2 T. flour	8 whole cloves
½ cup red wine vinegar and	1 medium onion, diced
½ cup water	1 tsp. thyme
Salt	

Preheat oven to 325°. Place flour in small (10 by 16 inch) plastic baking bag and shake until bag is well coated. Place bag in 2 inch deep roasting pan. Pour vinegar into bag and stir until well mixed with flour. Rub roast with salt and put into bag. Add bay leaf, cloves, onion and thyme around meat. Close bag with twist tie. If using a meat thermometer, insert thermometer through bag into center of meat. Make six ½ inch slits in top of bag near the tie. Cook 2 to 2½ hours or until internal temperature reaches 170° or meat is tender. The liquid in the bag is ready to use as gravy or thicken it with flour. Meat will not be especially juicy. Makes 6 to 8 servings.

Submitted by Cedar Mountain Ranch

BUFFALO STEW (WITHOUT TOMATO)

2 lbs. buffalo stew meat	1 large bay leaf
4 oz. diced pork (bacon or salt pork)	1½ tsp. salt
2 cups diced potatoes	½ tsp. black pepper
2 cups chopped celery	½ tsp. herb of your choice (thyme,
2 cups chopped onion	rosemary or marjoram)
2 chopped green peppers	3 to 4 cups water (divided)
1 T. chopped parsley	2 T. cornstarch
	2 T. water

In large skillet or electric fry pan, fry pork until crisp and remove from pan. Brown buffalo meat in pork fat and remove from pan. Cook the celery, onion, pepper and parsley 2 to 3 minutes in the remaining fat. Return the meat to the pan and add 2 cups water, bay leaf and seasonings. Stir up brownings from bottom of pan. Cover and simmer until meat is tender, about 2 hours. Stir in crisp pork, potatoes and 1 cup water (more if needed). When potatoes are cooked, thicken juices with cornstarch blended with small amount of water. Serve at once. Makes 6 to 8 servings.

Submitted by Cedar Mountain Ranch

HEARTY BUFFALO STEW (SLOW COOKER STYLE)

2 lbs. buffalo stew meat, cut in 1 inch cubes
5 carrots, cut in 1 inch pieces
1 large onion, cut in chunks
3 stalks celery, sliced
1 can (1 lb., 12 oz.) tomatoes

½ cup quick cooking tapioca
½ tsp. ground cloves
2 bay leaves
1 tsp. salt
½ tsp. pepper

Trim all fat from meat. Put all ingredients in slow cooker. Mix thoroughly. Cover and cook on low for 12 hours (high for 5 to 6 hours). Makes 4 to 6 servings.

Submitted by Cedar Mountain Ranch

BUFFALO FAJITAS

1 lb. buffalo skirt steak

MARINADE:

Juice of 2 to 3 limes
1 to 1½ tsps. garlic salt

½ tsp. pepper

(Or use any of the fajita marinades listed in this book)

GARNISHES:

1 large tomato, chopped
3 green onions, chopped
1 large green pepper, sliced

Guacamole
Sour cream
Salsa or green chilli, if desired

Pound meat into ¼ inch thickness. Place steak in plastic bag; sprinkle both sides of steak with lime juice, garlic salt and pepper. Tie bag securely and marinate in refrigerator 6 to 8 hours (or overnight). Drain marinade. Broil meat over medium high mesquite coals 2 to 3 minutes on each side. Carve into thin slices. Serve in warmed flour or corn tortillas. Add garnishes as desired. Makes 4 servings.

Submitted by Cedar Mountain Ranch

Note: Flank or round steak may be substituted, if desired. Round steak should be cut ½ inch thick. The word "fajita" means "little belt" or "girdle" or "cumberbund," and therefore refers specifically to the skirt steak. In current parlance, however, the word is used rather loosely to denote any piece of spiced, grilled meat served as described above.

ENCHILADA LAURIE AND TEXAS PRIME RED

2 bottles Texas Prime Red
4 lbs. ground beef or 4 lbs. chicken
   legs
1 T. black pepper
1 pint sour cream
1 pint cottage cheese

1 bottle (8 oz.) picante sauce
1 lb. grated cheddar cheese
1 pkg. (24 oz.) corn tortillas
Butter or margarine for frying
   tortillas

First put wine in the refrigerator to chill. Add pepper to ground beef and brown, or add to chicken and boil, then dice. In large bowl, blend together ingredients for the filling: the cooked meat, sour cream, cottage cheese, picante sauce and half the cheddar cheese. In small frying pan, melt a small tab of butter or margarine and fry each tortilla separately. Fry only enough to soften tortilla. Fill softened tortilla with some of the meat mixture, roll and place in casserole dish. Quickly start another tortilla and continue until dish is filled with enchiladas. Place the remainder of the filling on top of the rolled enchiladas. Sprinkle with the remaining cheese. Bake in 350° oven for 25 minutes or until it bubbles. Serve with chilled Texas Prime Red.

Submitted by Chateau Montgolfier Vineyards

MIXED GREEN SALAD

Lettuce
Romaine
Spinach
Red Cabbage

½ cup diced carrots
1 hardcooked egg
1 T. crisp cooked bacon, diced

Wash greens in ice cold water. Dry well and crisp in refrigerator. Cut in small pieces and mix together. Garnish with carrots, egg wedges, bacon, and diced red cabbage. Serve with Honey Mustard salad dressing on chilled plates.

Submitted by Chef A. Joseph Honey Mustard Dressing

FABULOUS CHEF'S JULIENNE SALAD

Mixed greens (romaine, chicory),
   chopped
1 oz. white meat of turkey,
   julienned
1 oz. ham, julienned

1 oz. Swiss cheese, julienned
Tomato wedges
Blue cheese
Watercress

Place greens in salad bowl and arrange julienned meat, cheese and tomato wedges over greens. Sprinkle with blue cheese and place a generous bouquet of watercress in center of salad. Serve with Honey Mustard Salad Dressing. ˙

Submitted by Chef A. Joseph Honey Mustard Dressing

MACARONI AND HAM SALAD

3 oz. elbow macaroni, raw
2 oz. cooked ham, julienned
½ cup celery, diced
¼ cup pimentos, diced
½ cup green peppers, diced and
  blanched

¼ cup onions, chopped finely
1 cup Honey Mustard Salad
Dressing
Head of lettuce, trimmed and
  separated

Cook macaroni and drain well. Have all ingredients well chilled. Combine all ingredients with Honey Mustard dressing and refrigerate for ½ hour before serving. Serve in lettuce cups.

Submitted by Chef a. Joseph Honey Mustard Dressing

CRAB MEAT AND AVOCADO SALAD

2 oz. crab meat
¼ cup celery, chopped
½ cup mayonnaise
1 avocado, ripe, peeled and
  chunked

1 T. pimentos, diced
1 T. Honey Mustard
1 cup chopped lettuce
⅛ tsp. salt
⅛ tsp. white pepper

Combine all ingredients together and serve with chips or other crispy foods.

Submitted by Chef A. Joseph Honey Mustard Dressing

CHEF'S POTATO SALAD

2 potatoes, cooked and diced in
  ¾ inch cubes
½ cup celery, diced finely
½ cup onions, minced
2 hard boiled eggs, chopped

1 oz. pimentos, drained and diced
1½ cups mayonnaise
½ cup Honey Mustard
Salt and pepper to taste

Combine all ingredients. Adjust seasoning if necessary.

Submitted by Chef A. Joseph Honey Mustard Dressing

INA'S PECAN PIE

1 cup Griffin syrup
½ cup sugar
3 T. oleo
Pinch of salt

3 eggs
⅛ tsp. vanilla
1 cup pecans

Heat syrup, sugar, oleo, salt to boiling point. Reduce heat and bubble for 5 minutes. Beat eggs slightly and add cooked mixture to eggs slowly. Add vanilla and pecans. Pour into pie shell. Bake at 350° for 50 minutes, or until done.

Submitted by The Clothes Line

SUGGESTED USES FOR CORSICANA DELUXE FRUIT CAKE

• Ice Cream Sandwich—Spread your favorite ice cream between two thin slices of DeLuxe Fruit Cake.

• Heat and Serve—Place slices of DeLuxe Fruit Cake in warming oven or in microwave oven (10 seconds only.) Serve with whipped cream.

• DeLuxe Continental Breakfast—Place buttered cake slices under broiler. Toast until butter melts. Serve warm with chilled juice and steaming hot coffee.

Submitted by Collin Street Bakery

BAKED CREOLE FISH

3 to 5 lbs. fish, whole red snapper   1 or 2 pints Cox's Creole Sauce
   or equivalent

Wash fish thoroughly and place in baking dish. Sprinkle with salt and pepper. Cover and bake at 300° for 1½ hours or until done. Drain off liquids and pour Creole Sauce over fish. Cover and cool slightly before serving. Serves 4 to 6.

Submitted by Cox's Relish Co.

CAJUN SHRIMP GUMBO

1 pint Cox's Gumbo Roux   1 small can oysters (opt.)
1 lb. shrimp, cooked and peeled   rice, as desired

Heat Gumbo Roux and shrimp in sauce pan. Serve over cooked rice. Serves 4 to 6. NOTE: Any cooked meat (chicken, beef, pork, fish or seafoods) makes an excellent gumbo.

Submitted by Cox's Relish Co.

SOUPER BOWL STEW

1 pint Cox's Stew Base   1 lb. beef, ground or cubed
1 pint water   egg noodles (opt.)
2 cups potatoes, diced

* Double all ingredients for 32. oz. size

Cook beef and drain excess fat. Add stew base, water and potatoes. Bring to a boil, reduce heat and simmer until potatoes are done. Delicious served with cornbread. Serves 4 to 6.

Submitted by Cox's Relish Co.

DELUXE SPICY MEAT LOAF

1 lb. ground beef
6 slices bread
water to moisten
2 whole eggs, beaten
1 medium onion, diced
1 medium bell pepper, diced

2 stalks celery, diced
4 T. cooking oil
2 T. Cox's BBQ Cooking Spice
1 tsp. garlic powder
½ pint Cox's Texas Hot Sauce

Moisten bread and squeeze out excess water. Add eggs, bread, cooking spice, garlic powder and hot sauce to ground beef and mix well. Saute onion, pepper and celery in cooking oil and add to meat mixture. Form into loaf, wrap in foil and place in baking dish. Bake 30 minutes at 350°, unwrap and bake 10 to 15 minutes to brown. Serves 4 to 6.

Submitted by Cox's Relish Co.

PO BOY'S BBQ

2 lbs. ground beef
1 pint Cox's BBQ Sauce

Buns

Brown ground beef and drain excess fat. Add BBQ sauce and simmer 10 minutes. Serve over toasted buns. Serves 4 to 6.

Submitted by Cox's Relish Co.

EGG DIP

12 boiled eggs
2 tsp. salt
1 medium onion, diced
3 stalks celery, diced

1 T. margarine
1 pint Cox's Texas Hot Sauce
2 medium tomatoes, diced

Dice eggs and sprinkle with salt. Saute onions and celery in margarine and add to eggs. Add Texas Hot Sauce and tomatoes and mix well. Chill and serve.

Submitted by Cox's Relish Company

GOLDEN GARDEN DIP

3 cups diced vegetables (green
  onions, celery, cucumbers,
  bell pepper, finely diced)

2 medium ripe tomatoes, diced
1 pint Cox's Texas Hot Sauce

Mix diced vegetables and tomatoes in mixing bowl. Stir in hot sauce. Chill and serve.

Submitted by Cox's Relish Company

SPICY AVOCADO DIP

3 ripe avocados
2 tsp sugar
1 medium onion
2 T. margarine
1 tsp. salt

2 medium ripe tomatoes
¼ tsp. black pepper
1 small lemon
1 cup Cox's Texas Hot Sauce

Peel and dice onion and saute in margarine. Peel and core avocados. Dice tomatoes. Mix Texas Hot Sauce and avocado and blend until creamy. Stir in juice from lemon, tomatoes and onion. Serve chilled.
NOTE: To soften avocados, place in microwave for 2 or 3 minutes.

Submitted by Cox's Relish Company

PARTY CHEESE DIP

1 pint Cox's Texas Hot Sauce   2 lbs. cheese, cubed

Pour hot sauce in saucepan and heat. Add cheese to hot sauce. Stir until cheese is melted. Serve warm.
EDITOR'S NOTE: Excellent served with Bellville Tortilla Chips.

Submitted by Cox's Relish Company

PINTO BEAN DIP

2 cups pinto beans, cooked   1 cup Cox's Texas Hot Sauce
1 cup juice from beans

Cook pinto beans and drain 2 cups. Mix in blender beans, juice and hot sauce until creamy. Serve warm with chips.

Submitted by Cox's Relish Company

POOR FARM HOT SAUCE

75 to 100 small red peppers (hot)
Water to cover
1 pod garlic

2 cups white vinegar
1 tsp. salt
1 T. sugar

Simmer the peppers and garlic until tender, about 1 or 2 hours. Drain and mash the peppers and garlic through a sieve. Mix this pulp with vinegar, salt and sugar. Let this simmer until the sauce thickens to the desired consistency. Yields ½ pint.

NOTE: This sauce is a HOT sauce lover's dream. Goes with eggs, soup, vegetables or anything that needs a little extra zest. This may be made in larger quantities and canned by sealing in sterilized jars and processing in boiling water bath for 5 minutes.

Submitted by David Comstock's Poor Farm

SUGGESTED USES FOR PEACH HONEY

- Use as a glaze for ham.
- Use as a fondue sauce.
- Spoon over ice cream.

- Spread on bread and top with cream.
- Use as a syrup for waffles.

Submitted by Das Peach Haus

SWEET & HOT HAM STEAK

1 center cut ham steak, at least
½ inch thick
1 to 2 T. oil, butter, drippings
(enough to coat skillet)

⅓ to ½ cup Dickie Davis'
Original Sweet and Hot
Sauce

Oil a skillet (preferably cast iron) lightly with oil, butter, margarine or drippings. Skillet may be sprayed with Pam or other vegetable spray. Put ham in cold skillet and set over medium heat. Cook until lightly browned on one side. Turn ham. Spread Sweet and Hot over ham while second side is browning. Turn ham once more and let sauce heat for 2 or 3 minutes. Turn out on warm platter.

Variation: Lift ham from skillet onto warm platter. Into sauce remaining in skillet, break 4 to 6 eggs. Cover skillet and allow eggs to set in sauce. Cut ham into large pieces and spoon egg with sauce on top of each piece.

Submitted by Editor for Dickie Davis' Original Sweet & Hot Sauce

PORK OR CHICKEN STEW "FRICASSE"

3 to 4 lb. chicken or pork
(seasoned)
2 large potatoes, quartered
(optional)
1 large onion
1 bell pepper

2 stalks celery
2 cloves garlic
½ cup green onion, chopped
¼ cup chopped parsley
5 T. Doguet's Roux
2 quarts water

Dissolve roux in water over medium heat, then boil ½ hour. Lower fire to medium heat and add all vegetables and meat. Cook until tender (about 1½ hours.) Add the green onions and parsley during the last 20 minutes of cooking. Serve over cooked Doguet's Rice.

Submitted by Doguet's Rice Milling Co.

ROAST BEEF
(Chuck, Shoulder, Blade or Rump)

1 beef roast, 4 to 5 lb.

salt and pepper

Rub roast with seasonings. Place roast on a rack in a pan and seal tightly with foil. Place pan in center of the oven. Turn oven on to 300°. Cook for 3 hours. Roast will be juicy and tender. Serve with your favorite vegetables.

Submitted by The Double L Ranch, Waelder, Tex.

PEACH GLAZED PORK RIBS

4 to 4½ lbs. pork ribs, cut into
serving pieces
1 to 1½ cups picante sauce

1½ cups peach preserves
¼ cup soy sauce

Place pork in shallow roasting pan with meaty sides up. Bake uncovered in 350° oven for 45 to 60 minutes. Heat picante, preserves and soy sauce to boiling. Stir constantly. Baste ribs several times while baking.

Submitted by E & B Orchards

BLUEBERRY CHEESECAKE PIE

1 pkg. (8 oz.) cream cheese
1 can Eagle brand condensed milk
⅓ cup lemon juice

1 tsp. vanilla
1 graham cracker crust

TOPPING:

2 cups fresh blueberries
½ cup sugar
2½ T. lemon juice

⅓ cup water
1½ T. cornstarch

Mix first four ingredients until smooth. Pour into pie crust and chill several hours. Combine ingredients for topping in a heavy saucepan. Bring to a boil. Boil until clear and thick. Cool before topping pie.

Submitted by E & B Orchards

BLUEBERRY INFORMATION AND TIPS

Blueberries freeze best if unwashed until ready to use. They will keep about 12 months frozen. They will keep up to two weeks in the refrigerator (also unwashed until ready to use.) Blueberries are a source of Vitamins A and C, calcium, phosphorous and potassium, and are only about 84 calories a cup. Blueberries with a light, powdery gray-blue color are what you want to look for when picking or buying blueberries. Berries picked before ripe will not continue to ripen. If a recipe calls for a can of blueberries, you may make your own by using:

2½ cups of fresh blueberries
1 T. corn starch

1½ tsp. lemon juice
⅛ cup water

Cook until thickened and clear. Cool before using as a substitute.

Submitted by EasTex Farms

32

BLUEBERRY CREAM CHEESE PIE

½ cup powdered sugar
1 (6 oz.) pkg. cream cheese (room temperature)
1½ to 2 cups softened Cool Whip

1 baked 9-inch pie shell or 1 (9 inch) graham cracker crust pie shell, baked

Blend powdered sugar and cream cheese until smooth. Add Cool Whip and blend all until smooth. Spread in pie shell and cover with the following blueberry sauce.

Sauce:

1 cup blueberries
⅔ cup water
1 cup sugar

3 T. cornstarch
⅓ cup water

Place blueberries and ⅔ cup water in saucepan and simmer for 3 minutes. Mix sugar and cornstarch together, then add ⅓ cup water. Combine this with the blueberries and boil for 1 minute, stirring constantly. Remove from heat, allow to cool 3 to 5 minutes. Pour over cream cheese mixture in pie shell and refrigerate.

Submitted by EasTex Farms

STIR FRY CHICKEN AND BEAN SPROUTS

2 chicken breasts, skinned, boned and thinly sliced
3 T. cornstarch
4 T. soy sauce
2 T. vegetable oil
1 pkg. Energy Produce broccoli (8 oz.)

¼ lb. mushrooms, sliced
1 pkg. Energy Sprouts bean sprouts
1 medium onion, sliced or chopped
1 cup chicken broth

Place chicken, cornstarch and soy sauce in a bowl and stir until chicken is thoroughly coated. Let stand 15 minutes. Heat oil in wok or skillet over high heat. Add chicken and stir-fry until browned. Remove chicken from wok. Add broccoli and onion to wok and stir-fry 2 minutes. Add mushrooms and bean sprouts. Return chicken to pan. Stir in chicken broth. Cover and cook on low heat for 5 minutes or until vegetables are tender crisp. Serve over rice. Serves 4.

Submitted by Energy Sprouts

OYSTER CAKE WITH EMERALD RIESLING BASIL CREAM SAUCE

¼ cup unsalted butter
⅓ cup minced garlic chives
½ cup yellow bell pepper, finely chopped
2 tsps. Mexican Mint Marigold, minced
2 eggs

10 oz. fresh oysters with liquor
1 cup sour cream
¾ cup blue cornmeal
¾ cup white flour
1¼ tsp. salt
1 T. sugar
1 T. baking powder

33

Saute garlic chives and yellow pepper in butter 3 to 5 minutes until soft. Remove from heat and stir in Mexican Mint Marigold. Drain oysters from liquor and reserve liquor (approximately ½ cup). Combine eggs, oyster liquor, sour cream, cornmeal, flour, pepper-butter mixture, salt, sugar and baking powder. Spread batter in well greased, hot baking pan (12 by 8 by 2 inches). Drop oysters (12 to 15)into batter and punch down slightly. Bake in 400° oven for 25 minutes. Garnish with garlic chives and serve with:

EMERALD RIESLING BASIL CREAM SAUCE

1 cup Fall Creek Vineyards Emerald Riesling	2 T. basil, minced
	4 T. fresh grated parmesan
2 T. unsalted butter	½ cup cream
2 tsps. garlic, minced	

Boil Emerald Riesling until reduced to approximately 2 tablespoons liquid. Saute garlic in butter. Add basil, parmesan and cream and simmer over low heat until slightly thickened. Add 2 T. reduced Emerald Riesling and whisk to combine. Serve immediately with oyster cake. Serves 8 to 10.

Submitted by Fall Creek Vineyards

SMOKED DUCK SALAD WITH EMERALD RIESLING MAYONNAISE AND FRIED CAYENNE PASTA

6 oz. smoked duck breast	1 small shallot, chopped
½ oz. red bell pepper, julienned	½ small clove garlic, chopped
½ oz. yellow bell pepper, julienned	2 T. chopped basil
	2 T. chopped cilantro
½ oz. carrot, julienned	1 tsp. chopped chives
½ oz. jicama, julienned	½ cup olive oil
½ oz. chayote, julienned	½ cup vegetable or corn oil
2 oz. red seedless grapes (peeled, if skins are too tannic)	¼ cup rendered duck fat
Sugar Snap Peas, to yield 2 oz. when shelled	3 T. chicken stock (if needed to thin mayonnaise)
1½ cups Fall Creek Vineyards Emerald Riesling	Additional salt and black pepper to taste
2 egg yolks	1 qt. peanut oil
1½ tsp. salt	4 oz. fresh cayenne pasta

Blanch shelled peas in boiling, salted water for 1 minute. Drain and plunge into ice water. When chilled, drain and set aside. Lengthwise, cut 8 thin slices from duck breasts and set aside for garnish. Cut remainder of duck into small cubes and place in mixing bowl with reserved peas, peppers, carrot, jicama, chayote and grapes. Set aside. In saucepan over high heat, reduce Riesling to 2 to 3 tablespoons. Let cool. Place wine and remaining ingredients (except fats and chicken stock and pasta) in blender and blend for 10 to 15 seconds. Combine olive oil, vegetable oil and rendered duck fat and slowly drizzle into blender with motor running. When thick and creamy, stop blending. Thin with chicken stock if necessary. In the mixing bowl, combine the mayonnaise and duck mixture. Season with salt and pepper and set aside while frying pasta. Heat peanut oil to 325°. (You should have 2 to 3 inches of oil in pan.) Fry pasta for 10 to 15 seconds and remove with slotted spoon or skimmer. Drain on paper towels. Place two reserved duck slices per plate on 4 plates. Arrange pasta on top of slices. Spoon salad on top of pasta.

Submitted by Fall Creek Vineyards
From Stephan Pyles, chef/owner Routh Street Cafe (Dallas)

ROAST PHEASANT WITH 1986 FALL CREEK EMERALD RIESLING-APPLE SAUCE AND WALNUT-COUNTRY HAM COMPOTE

3 pheasants (2½ lbs. each), wings
** and wishbones removed**
Salt to taste

The Mansion on Turtle Creek
** Pepper Mixture to taste**
4 T. peanut oil

Preheat oven to 400°. Generously season each bird inside and out with salt and pepper mixture. Heat oil in large, flat roasting pan large enough to hold three birds. Brown birds on all sides. Place pan in oven and roast pheasants for 20 to 25 minutes. Baste birds with pan juices at least twice during roasting. Remove pheasants from oven and allow birds to rest for at least 10 minutes before carving. When birds are cool enough to handle, remove leg and thigh quarters from breasts. Separate drumsticks and thighs at joint. Opposite skin side, make a slit along the length of the thigh bones and remove bones. Reserve boneless thighs. Use drumsticks and thigh bones for pheasant stock, if desired. Slice the boneless thighs and reconstruct in original shape. Keep warm. Next, remove the breast meat from the carcasses to make two boneless halves from each breast. Use the sharp point of a knife to cut between the meat and the bone starting at the widest part of the breast, separating each half. (Prior removal of the wishbone and wings makes this easier.) Peel off the skin and slice each breast half against the grain, starting with the thicker end. Slice very thin and keep in the shape of the breast halves. Ladle Riesling-Apple Sauce onto bottoms of each of 6 hot dinner plates. Arrange slices of Roasted Texas Pheasant from each breast half and a thigh to form a circle in the middle of each plate. Spoon a portion of Walnut-Country Ham Compote in the middle of each plate, so that it is surrounded by breast and thigh meat. Serve immediately.

Riesling-Apple Sauce

1 Red Delicious apple, cored and
  sliced thin
1 Granny Smith apple, cored and
  sliced thin
1 shallot, finely chopped
2 sprigs fresh thyme
¼ cup fine quality white port
  (preferably California)
1 cup pheasant demi-glace
1 cup 1986 Fall Creek Vineyards
  Emerald Riesling
4 raspberries
6 T. very cold unsalted butter cut
  into small pieces
Salt to taste
Juice of ½ lemon or to taste

In large saucepan over medium heat, combine sliced apples, shallot, thyme, port and pheasant demi-glace. Bring to a boil, reduce heat and simmer for about 20 minutes or until almost all liquid has evaporated. Remove from heat and set aside. Place Emerald Riesling in a medium sauce pan over medium heat, cook for about 8 minutes or until liquid is reduced by half. Combine apple mixture in saucepan with reduced wine. Add raspberries. Remove from fire and whisk in butter, piece by piece, to form an emulsion. Strain through a fine sieve and season to taste with salt and lemon juice. Keep warm. Do not allow mixture to come to a boil or emulsion will dissolve.

Walnut and Country Ham Compote

½ cup medium dice lean salt
  cured ham (from Missouri,
  Kentucky or Virginia or any
  other Smithfield type ham)
½ cup walnut halves
3 T. pure maple syrup
1 T. butter

Saute ham and walnuts in medium saute pan over medium heat for 2 minutes. Pour in maple syrup and stir to deglaze pan. Cook for 2 minutes. Whisk in butter, making sure it is incorporated into mixture. Keep warm. Serves 6. Advance preparation: Pheasants may be roasted up to 1 hour before serving and kept warm. Sauce may be prepared up to 1 hour before serving and kept warm.

Submitted by Fall Creek Vineyard
From Dean Fearing, chef, Mansion on Turtle Creek (Dallas)

TEXMATI APPLE CRISP

2 cups cooked Texmati Rice
1 can (20 oz.) sliced apples
1 T. lemon juice
1 cup brown sugar, divided
½ tsp. cinnamon
¼ tsp. salt
¾ cup flour
6 T. flour
½ cup chopped pecans
Whipped cream

Combine Texmati, apples, lemon juice, ½ cup brown sugar, cinnamon and salt in butter baking dish. Mix flour and remaining sugar. Cut in butter until mixture is crumbly. Stir in pecans. Sprinkle over rice mixture. Bake at 350° for 30 minutes. Serve warm, topped with whipped cream. Makes 6 servings.

Submitted by Farms of Texas Co.

TEXMATI AND CHICKEN STIR FRY

6 slices bacon, chopped
½ cup chopped onion
1 lb. chicken, boned, skinned and
  cut into strips
1 can (14 oz.) sliced mushrooms,
  drained
¼ cup diced pimentos

1 tsp. salt
1 tsp. pepper
1 T. soy sauce
1 cup snow peas
3 cups cooked Texmati Rice,
  white or brown

In large skillet or wok, saute bacon and onions until transparent. Add chicken and cook 5 to 10 minutes, until chicken is done but not browned. Stir in remaining ingredients. Heat thoroughly. Makes 6 servings.

Submitted by Farms of Texas Co.

BLUEBERRY COCONUT PIE

1 baked pastry shell (9 inch)
1 pkg. (3¾ oz) vanilla pudding
  and pie filling
1¾ cups milk

½ cup heavy cream, whipped
2 cups blueberries
1 cup coconut

Prepare pie filling according to package directions, but use only 1¾ cups milk. Cover and cool. Fold whipped cream and 1½ cups blueberries into the filling. Spoon into pie shell and cover with remaining berries. Sprinkle coconut over the berries.

Submitted by Fincastle Nursery and Farms

MICROWAVE PECAN BRITTLE

1 cup sugar
½ cup white corn syrup
1 cup pecans
½ tsp. salt

1 tsp. butter
1 tsp. vanilla
1 tsp. baking soda

In a 1½ qt. casserole, stir sugar, syrup, pecans and salt, mixing well. Microwave on HIGH for 6 to 9 minutes until light brown. Add butter and vanilla and stir well. Microwave on HIGH for 1 to 2 minutes more. Pecans will be light brown and syrup will be hot. Add baking soda and gently stir until light and foamy. Pour onto lightly buttered cookie sheet. Let cool 30 minutes to an hour. When cool, break into small pieces.

Submitted by The Frog House

BUTTERED PECAN ICE CREAM

2 cups chopped pecans
3 T. butter, melted
6 eggs
2 cups sugar
3 small boxes butter pecan
    pudding (instant)

1 large carton Cool Whip,
    softened
1½ tsps. vanilla
4 qts. milk

Saute pecans in butter in skillet for 5 minutes or until toasted. Beat eggs in large mixing bowl. Add sugar, graudally, mixing well. Pour in pudding mix, beating well. Stir in cool whip, cooled pecans and vanilla. Pour into a 1 ½ gallon freezer container. Add milk to fill line, stirring well. Freeze. Makes 1½ gallons.

Submitted by The Frog House

TASTY TEXAS BREAKFAST

8 eggs well beaten
½ cup grated cheese (longhorn,
    cheddar or Velveeta)

½ cup Galante Picante Sauce
    (hot, medium or mild)
1 T. chopped chives

Add all ingredients to eggs. Pour into hot non-stick skillet. Cook over medium heat until eggs are desired consistancy and cheese is melted. (Cooking longer will remove excess liquid.) Serve with link sausage, hot bisquits and cream gravy. Serves 4 hungry people.

Editors note: This recipe is also very good as a supper menu.

Submitted by Galante

SIX WEEKS BRAN MUFFINS

4 eggs
1 quart buttermilk
1 cup vegetable oil
1 box (15 oz.) raisin bran

3 cups sugar
5 cups flour
5 tsps. baking soda
2 tsps. salt

Mix eggs, buttermilk and oil.Add to remaining ingredients and mix well BY HAND. Paper line or grease muffin tins. Fill ⅔ full with batter and bake at 400° for 14 minutes. Yields 3 dozen. NOTE: This batter may be stored covered in refrigerator up to 6 weeks and used as desired.

Submitted by Gandy's Dairies

COMPANY COMIN' CASSEROLE

2 lbs. ground chuck
3 tsps. salt
4 tsps. sugar
½ tsp. pepper
2 cans (16 oz. each) tomatoes
2 cans (8 oz. each) tomato sauce
4 cloves garlic, chopped

1 pkg. (10 oz.) thin egg noodles
8 oz. cream cheese
2 cups sour cream
12 green onions, chopped with
    tops
2 cups grated sharp Cheddar
    cheese

Combine meat, salt, sugar, pepper, tomatoes, sauce and garlic. Simmer 10 to 15 minutes. Cook egg noodles. Drain. Combine hot noodles with cream cheese. Add sour cream and green onions. In a 4 quart casserole, layer noodles, meat mixture, and top with grated cheese. Bake at 325° for 40 minutes. Serves 8 to 10.

NOTE: Casserole may be made ahead of time and frozen.

Submitted by Gandy's Dairies

FESTIVE FROZEN CRANBERRY SALAD

1 can (16 oz.) cranberry sauce
1 carton (8 oz.) sour cream
1 cup miniature marshmallows
1 can (8 oz.) crushed pineapple
   (drained)

1 banana, sliced into small pieces
½ cup chopped nuts
½ cup sugar

Place cupcake papers in muffin tins. Mix all ingredients together and fill liners ⅔ full. Cover with foil and plastic wrap and freeze. Serves 12.

Submitted by Gandy's Dairies

LEMON SOUR CREAM PIE

1 baked 9 inch pie shell
1 cup sugar
3 T. cornstarch
1 cup milk
3 egg yolks, beaten
¼ cup lemon juice

1 T. grated lemon rind
⅓ cup butter
1 cup sour cream
½ pint whipping cream, whipped
1 to 2 T. sugar

Combine sugar and cornstarch. Add milk, egg yolks, lemon juice, rind and butter. Cook over medium heat until thick. Cool. When cool, add sour cream and blend. Pour into baked pie shell. Refrigerate for several hours. Top with whipped cream (sweetened with sugar) before serving.

Submitted by Gandy's Dairies

SPRINGTIME SALAD

1 carton (24 oz.) cottage cheese
1 box (6 oz.) lime gelatin
1 large can (15 oz.) crushed
   pineapple, drained

1 cup chopped pecans
1 carton (8 oz.) whipped topping

Sprinkle gelatin over cottage cheese. Blend in whipped topping, pineapple and nuts. Pour into a mold or bowl and chill for at least 2 hours before serving. Serves 6 to 8.

Submitted by Gandy's Dairies

EASY HOLIDAY EGGNOG CREAM PIE

1½ cups graham cracker crumbs (about 20 crackers)
3 T. sugar
⅓ cup Quality Chekd butter
4 cups Quality Chekd Eggnog
¼ cup cornstarch
2 T. Quality Chekd butter, softened

Mix crumbs, sugar and butter. Press mixture firmly into 9 inch pie pan covering bottom and sides. Bake 10 minutes in 350° oven. Cool. Blend eggnog and cornstarch in saucepan. Cook over medium heat, stirring constantly, until mixture thickens and boils. Boil and stir 1 minute. Remove from heat, blend in butter. Immediately pour into baked pie shell. Press plastic wrap onto filling. Chill pie thoroughly, at least 2 hours. Serve pie with whipped cream or sprinkle with shaved dark chocolate.

Submitted by Gandy's Dairies

CLAM COTTAGE CHEESE MOLD

1 can (8 oz.) minced clams
1 envelope unflavored gelatin
1¼ cups Quality Chekd 2% milk
½ tsp. Worchestershire sauce
½ tsp. salt
3 drops Tabasco
Dash grated nutmeg
⅔ cup Quality Chekd cottage cheese
1 T. chopped green pepper
½ T. onion flakes

Drain clams, reserving ½ cup liquid. Sprinkle gelatin on liquid to soften in saucepan. Place over low heat and stir until gelatin dissolves. Remove from heat and add milk, Worshestershire sauce, salt, Tabasco and nutmeg. Chill just until mixture thickens. Add clams, cottage cheese, green pepper and onion flakes. Turn into 2½ cup mold or small loaf pan. Chill until firm. Unmold to serve.

Submitted by Gandy's Dairies

COUNTRY CREAM OF CORN SOUP

1 quart Quality Chekd milk
½ cup Quality Chekd half and half
2 ears cooked corn on the cob (should yield 1 cup, grated) or
1 can (8 oz.) cream style corn
1 small onion, coarsely chopped
3 T. butter
1½ T. flour
½ tsp. salt
¼ tsp. freshly ground pepper
½ tsp. cayenne pepper
Croutons
¼ cup chopped celery

In a saucepan, heat the milk and light cream. Grate the corn until very fine. Saute chopped onion in 1 T. butter. In a large flameproof casserole, melt 2 T. butter. Stir in the flour and blend until mixed. Pour in heated milk and cream. Add onion, corn, salt and pepper and cayenne. Heat until boiling point. Serve in individual soup bowls and garnish with croutons and chopped celery.

Submitted by Gandy's Dairies

TEXAS RED WINE CHILI

1 bottle TEXAS RED WINE
1 lb. chili meat, cubed
1 large onion, chopped
3 cups cooked pinto beans
2 cans (16 oz. ea.) tomatoes

1½ to 2 T. chili powder
2 tsp. salt
¼ tsp. black pepper
1 clove garlic, minced
1 tsp. cumin

Marinate chili meat in enough wine to cover 3 to 4 hours or overnight in refrigerator. Drain. Brown meat in large skillet. Add remaining ingredients. Cover and simmer slowly for 1 to 2 hours. Serves 4.

Submitted by Guadalupe Valley Winery

TEXAS RED SANGRIA

2 bottles GUADALUPE VALLEY
TEXAS RED WINE
16 oz. ginger ale
16 oz. orange juice

¾ cup lemon juice
2 lemons
2 limes
3 oranges

Mix wine and juices in large punch bowl. Thinly slice fruit and add to sangria. Serve chilled over ice.

TEXAS RED WINE also makes a thirst quenching spritzer. Just mix one part wine to two parts uncola or ginger ale. Serve over ice with a twist of lime.

Submitted by Guadalupe Valley Winery

HELL ON THE RED CHICKEN

1 chicken 3 to 4 lbs. or same
amount of chicken parts
½ tsp. garlic powder
1 large onion, chunked

1 large bell pepper, cut in 1 inch
pieces
1 cup Hell on the Red party dip
(hot or mild)

Split chicken down back and flatten to place in casserole dish or place chicken parts in casserole dish. Mix remaining ingredients and pour over chicken. Bake in 325° oven for 45 minutes or until chicken is tender. Serve with rice.

Editor's note: Casserole dish may be covered until last 15 minutes of cooking to prevent excess drying.

Submitted by Hell on the Red

HILL COUNTRY SPRITZER

Fill a glass half full with ice cubes. Add Utopia Sparkling Water flavor of your choice (lime, lemon, cherry or orange) or use the unflavored variety. Garnish with appropriate fruit—a lemon slice, lime slice, orange slice or cherry slice.

Submitted by Hill Country Spring Water of Texas, Inc.

HONEY SWEETNIN' FOR TEA

5 cups water   3 cups honey

Bring water to full boil. Dissolve honey in water. Do NOT boil honey. Keep in refrigerator.

OTHER TIPS FOR HONEY USES:

When substituting honey for sugar in cake and cookie recipes, a general rule is to reduce the amount of liquid ¼ cup for each cup of honey used to replace sugar.

Cakes and cookies made with honey are noted for their keeping qualities. The ability of honey to absorb and retain moisture and thus retard the drying out and staling of baked goods is of great importance to the homemaker who wishes to do her baking in advance.

Submitted by Ruth Weaver, Howard Weaver & Sons

RUTH'S HONEY PECAN PIE

2 uncooked pie shells   3 tablespoons melted oleo
6 eggs   2 cups chopped pecans
1½ cups sugar   2 tsp. vanilla
1 cup honey

Beat eggs until well blended. Add sugar, honey and blend well. Add cooled oleo and vanilla, mixing until blended. Spread nuts in bottom of pie shells. Pour filling over nuts. Place in oven preheated to 350°. Reduce heat to 325°. Bake 50 to 60 minutes.

Submitted by Ruth Weaver, Howard Weaver & Sons

BAVARIAN BRATWURST WITH SAUERKRAUT

1 jar (32 oz.) sauerkraut   4 juniper berries
6 slices bacon   Hubbell Bavarian Brand
1 medium onion, chopped   Bratwurst
1 tsp. caraway seeds   Water
2 bay leaves   1 T. oil

Rinse sauerkraut. Cut bacon into strips and fry in medium size pot. Add chopped onion to bacon and fry until transparent. Add rinsed sauerkraut and seasonings. Mix, add water and bring to boil. Turn heat down, cover, and let simmer for two hours. Check occasionally to make sure there is enough liquid. Sauerkraut tastes better the next day. Heat bratwurst in hot water for about 10 minutes (do not boil). Then brown in frying pan with oil. Serve sausages with sauerkraut and potato salad and mustard.

Submitted by Hubbell & Sons

BAVARIAN POTATO SALAD AND BRATWURST

6 medium potatoes
6 slices bacon
⅛ of a medium onion, chopped
¾ tsp. salt or to taste
6 T. white vinegar or to taste

Fresh ground black pepper
¼ to ½ cup hot water
Hubbell Bavarian Bratwurst
Water
1 T. oil

Cook potatoes till tender, peel and cut into thin slices. Cut bacon once lengthwise, then into squares. Fry in small saucepan, then pour with about half of the bacon grease over the potatoes. Add onion, salt, vinegar, pepper and water. Mix and serve hot. Or let cool to room temperature, mix again, taste if seasoning needs to be adjusted. Heat bratwurst in hot water for about 10 minutes. (Do not boil.) Then brown in frying pan with oil. Serve with sauerkraut, potato salad and mustard.

Submitted by Hubbell & Sons

LUNCHBOX BROWNIES

¼ cup margarine or butter
¾ cup shortening
¾ cup cocoa
2 cups Imperial granulated sugar
4 eggs, beaten

1 tsp. vanilla
1½ cups all purpose flour
1 tsp. baking powder
1 tsp. salt
1 cup chopped nuts

Melt margarine and shortening in a large saucepan over low heat; stir in cocoa. Remove from heat and add sugar, eggs and vanilla, mixing well. Combine flour, baking powder and salt; stir into chocolate mixture. Add nuts and mix well. Spread in well-greased 13 by 9 by 2 inch baking pan. Bake at 350° for 30 to 35 minutes. Cool, cut into 2-inch squares. Yields approximately 2 dozen brownies.

Submitted by Imperial Sugar

ALMOND PUMPKIN CHARLOTTE

1 cup almonds
3 T. honey
2 T. plus ⅓ cup dark rum
1½ pkgs. (3 oz. ea.) ladyfingers, split but not separated into individual fingers.
2 envelopes unflavored gelatin.
⅔ cup light brown sugar, lightly packed

4 eggs, separated
⅔ cup milk
1 can (1 lb.) pumpkin
1 tsp. Janet's Own Pumpkin Pie Spice
½ pint (1 cup) heavy or whipping cream

Heat oven to 350°. Spread almonds in ungreased baking pan. Bake 10 minutes or until toasted. Cool. Reserve 15 almonds for garnish. In food processor, coarsely chop remaining almonds. Remove half of the chopped almonds. Continue to whirl almonds in the processor until they are ground. Place ground almonds on a sheet of waxed paper. In small bowl, combine honey and 2 T. rum. Brush ladyfingers on both sides with rum mixture; dip into ground almonds to coat. Line the side of an 8-inch spring-form pan with ladyfingers, rounded sides out. Line bottom with remaining ladyfingers, cutting them to fit if necessary. In 2 quart pan, combine gelatin and ½ cup of the sugar. Stir in egg yolks until well mixed. Stir in milk and ½ cup of rum. Stir over low heat to make a soft custard, about 10 minutes. Remove from heat. Stir in pumpkin and pumpkin spice. Refrigerate just until cool but not set. In large bowl with mixer, beat egg whites to form soft peaks. Gradually beat in remaining ½ cup sugar to form stiff peaks. In small bowl, whip heavy cream. Gently fold pumpkin mixture and whipped cream into egg white mixture. Fold in chopped almonds. Pour into lined pan. Chill at least 6 hours or overnight. (Can be made up to 3 days ahead; cover top with plastic wrap.) To serve, remove sides of pan. Garnish top with whole almonds.

ENCHILADA EXPRESS
TIPO MEXICANO/LAID OUT LIKE LASAGNA

1 clove garlic	8 oz. tomato sauce
½ diced bell pepper	10 oz.Monterey Jack cheese
½ diced onion	1 doz. fresh corn tortillas
4 T. safflower oil	Safflower oil
3 T. Janet's Own Enchilada Spices	

Saute garlic, bell pepper and onion in 4 T. oil. Add Janet's Own Enchilada Spices and tomato sauce. Cook 15 minutes. Remove from burner. Grate cheese and mix with a small bit of chopped onion. Heat safflower oil. Dip tortillas in hot oil until soft. Dip same tortillas into cooled sauce. Lay tortillas flat in baking dish. Sprinkle cheese and onion mix. Cover with another tortilla dipped in oil and sauce. Repeat and stack like lasagna. Cover top layer liberally with cheese and sauce. Bake at 350° for 30 minutes.

Variation: Cooked boned chicked may be added between layers, too.

TACO SABROSO
(The Delicious Taco)

½ small chopped onion	3 T. safflower oil
½ chopped bell pepper	1 T. Janet's Own Taco Sabroso
1 lb. lean ground beef or ground round	Seasoning

Saute onion and bell pepper in oil. Add lean beef and cook 15 minutes. Drain all excess oil and add Janet's Own Taco Sabroso Seasoning. Cook an additional 10 minutes. Stuff into taco shells (bought or homemade). Stuff more with diced tomatoes, lettuce and a little raw onion, chopped. Serve with Janet's Salsa Con Sabor.

SALSA CON SABOR

BASIC:

2 T. Janet's Own Salsa con Sabor   2 T. safflower oil
1 can (8 oz.) tomato sauce

Saute Janet's Own Salsa con Sabor in safflower oil. Add tomato sauce. Cook at low heat for 15 minutes.

CHUNKY:

½ onion, diced   1 large ripe tomato, diced
½ bell pepper, diced

Saute vegetables in oil. Add Janet's Own Salsa spices and 8 oz. tomato sauce. Cook at low heat for 15 minutes.

HOT: Prepare Chunky Salsa con Sabor as above. Dice one fresh serrano or jalapeno pepper and cook with salsa. If you are brave, leave all the seeds intact. Serve chilled sauce for salsa con tortilla chips or serve hot with Huevos Rancheros.

Submitted by Janet's Own Home Sweet Home

WINTER WARMER

2 quarts apple cider   1½ cups pineapple juice
1 T. Janet's Own Winter Warmer

Combine ingredients and simmer for 30 minutes. Strain and serve hot.

Submitted by Janet's Own Home Sweet Home

CAJUN SEASONING FOR BLACKENED FISH OR CHICKEN

2 lbs. of fish fillets or boneless   1 cup of butter, melted
  chicken breasts ½ to ¾ inch   1 tsp. Janet's Own Cajun
  thick   Seasoning

Brush both sides of meat with melted butter (use rest of butter in pan.) Sprinkle both sides of meat with Janet's Own Cajun Seasoning. Heat a cast iron skillet over high heat. Add butter. Cook meat on each side for 2 to 3 minutes, being careful when turning. The meat will look charred. There will be some smoke. This recipe may be cooked outdoors, if preferred.

Submitted by Janet's Own Home Sweet Home

CURRY IN A HURRY

½ cup cream   ½ cup mayonnaise
½ cup plain yogurt   2 T. chopped onion
2 medium stalks chopped celery   3 oz. slivered almonds
4 apples, cored and sliced   1 cooked, diced chicken
2 T. Janet's Own Curry in a Hurry

Mix cream, mayonnaise and yogurt. Stir in 2 T. Janet's Curry in a Hurry. Add cold chicken, onion and celery. Garnish with almonds and sliced apples. Serve chilled.

Submitted by Janet's Own Home Sweet Home

HERB BUTTER AUX FRESH HERBS

4 oz. softened butter	3 T. Janet's Own Fresh Herb
1 T. fresh lemon juice	Bouquet
Freshly ground black pepper	

Cream the butter and mix it a bit at a time with lemon juice. Blend Janet's Own Fresh Herb Bouquet into butter. Sprinkle with coarsely ground black pepper. Serve chilled on fresh bread or use on steamed vegetables, omelettes or new potatoes.

Submitted by Janet's Own Home Sweet Home

SATAY CHICKEN SALAD

2 whole chicken breasts, boned, skinned and cut in half	4 cups shredded romaine lettuce
Soy sauce	1 cup fresh or canned bean sprouts, rinsed and drained
⅓ cup La Martinique True French Vinaigrette	½ cup shredded carrot
¼ cup Pace Picante Sauce	½ cup thinly sliced celery
½ tsp. sugar	½ cup coarsely chopped dry roasted peanuts
¼ tsp. ground ginger	

Simmer chicken in water to cover, seasoned with 2 Tablespoons soy sauce, about 10 minutes or until tender and cooked through. Drain and set aside. Combine vinaigrette, picante sauce, 1 Tablespoon soy sauce, sugar and ginger in small saucepan. Heat thoroughly, stirring frequently. Arrange lettuce, sprouts, carrot and celery on a large platter or 4 salad plates. Thinly slice chicken. and arrange over vegetables. Sprinkle with peanuts. Drizzle with warm dressing. Makes 4 servings.

Submitted by La Martinique Restaurant Dressing

SASSY SPINACH SALAD

1 12 oz. bag spinach, torn into bite size pieces	½ small red onion, thinly sliced, separated into rings
1 cup thin mushroom slices	¼ cup La Martinique Original Poppy Seed Dressing
4 crisply cooked bacon sliced, crumbled	¼ tsp. dry mustard

Combine spinach, mushrooms, bacon and onion in salad bowl. Toss lightly. Combine dressing and mustard in small saucepan, mixing well.Heat thoroughly. Pour hot dressing over salad. Toss lightly and serve immediately. Serves 6.

Submitted by La Martinique Restaurant Dressings

MUSHROOM RICE SALAD

Cook amount of rice desired (1 cup raw rice equals three to four cups cooked rice.) Cool. Add fresh or canned mushroom slices, halved, blanched or frozen pea pods or sugar snap peas and chopped red pepper to cooked rice. Toss with La Martinique Blue Cheese Vinaigrette. Refrigerate at least 4 hours. Toss before serving.

Submitted by La Martinique Restaurant Dressings

LANTANA HOLIDAY STUFFING

2 packages cornbread mix
1 lb. bulk pork sausage
4 plain white bread slices
½ cup chopped onion
2 large cloves garlic, minced
½ cup chopped celery and leaves
¼ cup chopped parsley
1 T. poultry seasoning

6 small fresh mushrooms, sliced
or
1 jar sliced mushrooms
3 T. Lantana all purpose
   seasoning
1 can cream of chicken soup
2½ cups chicken broth

Prepare cornbread mix as directed on package. Let cool and crumble in large bowl. Pan saute pork sausage and add onion and garlic, cool and add to cornbread. Crumble plain white bread, add remaining ingredients and mix thoroughly. If using a 12 lb. turkey, wash thoroughly, baste with butter and sprinkle with Lantana seasoning. Let sit overnight. Place stuffing inside turkey and place in shallow pan. Bake at 325° for 4 hours. If not using turkey, saute sausage, onion, garlic, celery and mushrooms before adding to cornbread mixture. Place in a 2½ quart casserole dish and bake 45 minutes at 350°.

Submitted by Lantana South Texas All Purpose Seasoning

LANTANA SPECIAL OCCASION CHEESE SPREAD

2 8-oz. packages cream cheese
2 oz. blue cheese crumbled
4 oz. sharp cheddar cheese, grated
2 T. minced onion (flakes)

3 T. olives with pimentos,
   chopped
1 T. Worcestershire
2 T. Lantana seasoning

Cream together blue cheese and cream cheese. Add grated cheddar cheese. Add remaining ingredients in order and blend thoroughly. Form into a ball or mound in a bowl or on a platter. Surround with favorite crackers and sprinkle with Lantana seasoning for extra flavor and color.

Submitted by Lantana South Texas All Purpose Seasoning

LANTANA DEVILED EGGS

1 dozen hardboiled eggs
1½ T. pickle relish
2 T. chopped pimentos or olive
  with pimentos
1 T. chopped onions
1½ tsp. Lantana

½ tsp. celery seed or celery
  chopped finely
½ cup mayonnaise or salad
  dressing
1 tsp. French prepared mustard

Halve whole eggs and mash yolks with fork. Add remaining ingredients and mix thoroughly. Place mixture into halved egg white shells. Sprinkle with Lantana seasoning mix.

Submitted by Lantana South Texas Whole Food Seasoning

LANTANA FRIED MUSHROOMS

1 lb. mushrooms
1 can Progresso Italian bread
  crumbs
⅓ cup grated Parmesan cheese

1 T. Lantana seasoning
¾ cup flour
1 egg beaten with 4 T. water

Clean mushrooms, toss with Lantana and flour, coating well. Dip in egg mixture, then in breadcrumbs mixed with cheese. Deep fry until brown.

Serve with the following sauce:

16 oz sour cream
1 T. cream style horseradish

1 T. Lantana seasoning

Submitted by Lantana South Texas Whole Food Seasoning

SOUTH TEXAS BRISKET

5 to 6 lb. boneless brisket
Lantana all purpose seasoning
1 cup red wine

2 to 3 T. brown sugar
2 to 3 pickled jalapenos (sliced)

Cover all sides of brisket with Lantana and place fat side up in heavy foil (enough to tightly seal later). Place in baking pan, spread brown sugar evenly over brisket and top with jalapenos. Pour red wine in the foil (not on the brisket), seal foil tightly and balke at 325° for 3 to 4 hours.

Note: Jalapenos may be altered according to taste.

Submitted by Lantana South Texas All Purpose Seasoning

CHICKEN SAUSAGE GUMBO

1½ lbs Laxson sausage
1 large chicken, cut in pieces
5 T. oil or lard
6 T. flour
2 large onions, minced
1 bell pepper, chopped
1 cup chopped celery
3 cloves garlic, minced
2½ qts. chicken stock

½ tsp. thyme
3 bay leaves
⅛ tsp. powdered cloves
⅛ tsp. powdered allspice
¼ tsp. cayenne pepper
½ tsp. basil
salt and pepper to taste
½ cup chopped green onions
file powder (optional)

Fry chicken in oil until brown. Next, fry the sausage for 4 or 5 minutes. reserve the chicken and sausage. To the oil left in the pot, add the flour and slowly cook to a nice brown. Place in the pan the onions, bell pepper and celery. Saute until vegetables are limp. Add the chicken stock, garlic, thyme, bayleaves, cloves, allspice, cayenne and basil. Carefully add salt and black pepper. Let this mixture slowly simmer for at least 40 minutes. Then add the chicken and sausage. Cook til the chicken is tender.

Submitted by Laxson Provision Company

SAUSAGE JAMBALAYA

1 or 1¼ lbs. Laxson sausage
2 large onions, chopped
½ cup finely chopped celery
1 bell pepper, chopped
1 large can tomatoes
2 bay leaves
½ tsp. basil
½ tsp thyme
½ tsp. chili powder

4 cloves garlic, chopped
1 can beef consomme
2 cans water
Salt, black pepper and Tabasco
   to taste
2 cups raw rice
½ cup finely chopped shallots
2 T. minced parsley

Slice sausage into small pieces, then brown in a deep frying pan or Dutch oven. Remove meat and add onions, celery and pepper to the pot. Saute until tender. Mix in tomatoes thoroughly. Add bay leaves, basil, thyme, chili powder and garlic. Mix well and add beef consomme and water. Let simmer about 40 minutes. Return sausage to pot. Add salt, pepper and Tabasco to taste. Add rice. Cover pot and allow the mixture to cook slowly, stirring occasionally. As the rice begins to absorb the mixture, the jambalaya may get too dry. If so, add a little more water. Cook until rice is tender. Just before serving, stir shallots and parsley into the jambalaya. Let set for 10 minutes. Serves 4 to 6.

Submitted by Laxson Provision Co.

SHRIMP WITH MUSHROOMS

1 lb. headless, fresh shrimp, cleaned and peeled

30 to 40 fresh mushrooms, washed

MARINADE:

1 oz. salad oil
1 oz. olive oil
Juice of one lime
1 T. wine vinegar

1 tsp. Old San Antonio Fajita Seasoning
1 T. mild jalapenos, diced (for flavor without heat)

Place marinade in a bowl, add shrimp and mushrooms and cover. Place in refrigerator for 4 hours. Preheat a saute pan (pan is hot when drop of marinade sizzles.) Place the shrimp and mushrooms along with some of the marinade in pan and cook together, stirring constantly for 4 to 5 minutes. Add marinade as needed to keep cooking surface wet.

Submitted by Lazy Susan Foods (Old San Antonio)

OLD SAN ANTONIO ENCHILADAS

salad oil
1 onion, finely chopped
1 jar (8 oz.) Old San Antonio Salsa Verde
1 can (6 oz.) tomato paste

2 cups chopped cooked chicken
½ tsp. Old San Antonio Fajita Seasoning
½ lb. cheddar cheese, grated
1 package (15) corn tortillas

Saute onion in 2 T. oil in large skillet, about 5 minutes. Add remaining ingredients except cheese and tortillas. Simmer covered, 10 minutes. Heat ½ inch salad oil in small skillet until hot. Dip tortillas one at a time into oil, about 15 seconds, until limp. DO NOT LET THEM BECOME CRISP. Drain. Top each tortilla with 3 to 4 tablespoons filling. Roll up. Place seam side down in a greased 3 qt. shallow baking dish. Pour either the Old San Antonio Salsa Verde or Enchilada Sauce over enchiladas. Sprinkle with cheese. Bake at 350°, uncovered for 15 to 20 minutes or until hot. Makes 15 enchiladas.

VARIATION for cheese enchiladas: Prepare the tortillas as stated above and substitute the chicken filling with mild cheddar cheese, grated. Cover with Old San Antonio Picante Sauce (if you like them hot) or Old San Antonio Enchilada Sauce for a mild topping.

Submitted by Lazy Susan Inc.

"PAISANO" WESTERN STYLE BARBECUE
(FOR CHICKEN, RIBS OR BEEF)

Prepare broilers or meats. Sprinkle with paprika, salt, black pepper, onion powder and garlic powder. Wrap meats in foil. Place in refrigerator and leave over night.

Next day, arrange in baking dish, cover with foil. Bake at 475° for 20 minutes. Baste with Paisano Original Bar-B-Que Sauce. Reduce heat to 325° and bake for 45 minutes or longer until tender. Baste occasionally with the sauce. This may also be cooked on a regular barbecue pit.

Submitted by L-C Food Products

KARON'S GOLLY TAMALE PIE

2 cups chili
1 cup chopped onion
1 can (10 oz.) corn kernels,
  drained
½ cup variety baking mix

1 cup milk
3 eggs
1 cup shredded Monterey Jack
  cheese

In a 9 inch deep dish pie plate spread chili. Sprinkle onions or corn (or both) evenly over chili. Mix baking mix with milk and eggs and pour over all. Bake at 400° for 40 minutes. If desired, during last 10 minutes of baking, sprinkle cheese over top of pie. Let pie settle 10 minutes before cutting.

Submitted by Lone Star Chef

SUGGESTED USES FOR CHILI FIXIN'S

• Use your Chili Fixin' packet for a Tex-Mex meat loaf. Just add to your favorite recipe and cook.
• Spoon chili over eggs — good for breakfast or supper.
• Mix chili with noodles, spaghetti or macaroni. Or spoon over red beans or sometimes with rice. Nice and easy.
• Garnish chili with raw onions and cheese. Or try sour cream and lime wedges.
• Add chili to a hot dog for a chili dog. Or to a hamburger for a chili-burger.
• Chili over Fritos, cheese and onions makes Frito pie.
• Don't discard leftover chili (if there is any.) Chili is always better the second day. Freezes well, too.

Submitted by Lone Star Chef

FRESH FRUIT COBBLER

½ cup butter
2 cups sugar, divided
¾ cup all purpose flour
2 tsps. baking powder

Dash salt
¾ cup milk
2 cups sliced fruit — apples,
  apricots or peaches

Melt butter in a 2 quart baking dish. Combine 1 cup sugar, flour, baking powder and salt. Add milk. Stir until mixed. Pour batter over butter in baking dish, but DO NOT STIR. Combine fruit and remaining one cup sugar, spoon over batter. DO NOT STIR. Bake at 350° for 1 hour. Yield 6 to 8 servings.

Submitted by Maxwell Orchards

CHARCOALED SHRIMP

1¼ lbs. large shrimp (allow 3 to 4 cloves garlic
 approximately 12 per person) Paprika
1 bottle (8 oz.) Italian salad
 dressing

Clean shrimp. Place in a large shallow baking dish and pour Italian dressing over until shrimp are covered. Add garlic cloves. Chill for 2 to 24 hours. Thread shrimp onto metal skewers. Sprinkle with paprika. When coals are very hot, cook shrimp about 7 to 8 minutes per side. Cooking time depends on the size of the shrimp. Serve immediately. Or replace in dish with marinade and place in low oven to keep warm. The paprika will make them brown nicely.

Submitted by W.R. Mickle Inc.

SAUERKRAUT

1 quart Millie's Kountry Kitchen 2 T. flour
 Sauerkraut ½ cup water
3 T. bacon drippings

Add ½ cup water to sauerkraut and heat thoroughly on medium heat for 10 minutes. In another pan, add 3 T. bacon drippings and two level teaspoons of flour and saute for 1 to 2 minutes. Add mixture to sauerkraut and heat thoroughly for 2 to 3 minutes.

Submitted by Millie's Kountry Kitchen Inc.

SUGGESTED USES FROM MISS MARY

• Sweet and Sour Pepper Jelly: Use as a glaze for chicken. Try on a roast beef sandwich.
• Corn Relish: Drain and toss in potato salad.
• Chow Chow: Great on hot dogs. Or mix in tuna fish salad.
• Texas Caviar: What else? Perfect for New Year's Day. Chill and toss with any bean salad. Or mix with Miss Mary's Hot Sauce for a dip.
• Strawberry Horseradish: Try as an accompaniment to fried chicken or steak fingers. Miss Mary loves her strawberry horseradish as a dip for cold boiled shrimp.

Submitted by Miss Mary's Fine Foods

SUGGESTED USES FOR CHILE CON QUESO

• Heat and pour over nacho chips, season with jalapeno peppers to taste. Also make individual nacho chips.
• Heat and pour over fresh or cooked vegetables.
• Mix with eggs to make a delicious Mexican omelette.
• Use as a sauce for tacos, fajitas, burgers, steaks, chicken, enchiladas, tamales, hot dogs, etc.

Submitted by Monterey House

SUGGESTED USES FOR HOT PICANTE SALSA

- As a dip for chips.
- Use on hamburgers, steak, guacamole, chicken, etc.
- Mix with other foods to spice up flavor.
- Mix with sour cream for a dip.

Submitted by Monterey House

SUGGESTED USES FOR PICANTE BEAN DIP

- Heat and pour over nacho chips.
- Use as a party dip for chips and vegetables.
- Use as a side dish for any meal.

Submitted by Monterey House Inc.

TEXAS CHAMPAGNE SORBET

1 bottle (about 3 cups of chilled champagne)

1½ cups simple syrup — half water and half sugar, boiled, dissolved and chilled.

Pour champagne and syrup into ice cream maker and freeze 30 minutes. Makes 5 cups. Alcohol sorbet defrosts quickly so leave it in the machine or ice cream maker until moments before serving. Serve as part of a long dinner — in between courses — or for dessert with fresh stawberries or any other fresh berry. (Try a Texas favorite — fresh dewberries. In the winter, pour over fresh frozen peaches, still icy.)

EDITOR'S NOTE: For this recipe use Moyer Texas Champagne of New Braunfels which produces two champagne types — Brut Especial and Brut Natural. Either type will work quite well in the sorbet — and for drinking.

Submitted by Editor for Moyer Texas Champagne

TOMATO AND MOZZARELLA SALAD

½ lb. fresh mozzarella cheese
2 ripe tomatoes
Fresh basil leaves

Salt, freshly ground black pepper
Olive oil

Slice Mozzarella into ¼ inch or ½ inch slices. Slice tomatoes. Alternate slices of each on a platter and then season with salt and pepper and a little olive oil. Decorate with fresh basil leaves. Serves two.

This classic dish is good for a light lunch, a buffet or a summer first course.

Submitted by The Mozzarella Company

TWO TEXAS CHEESE SALADS

SALAD NUMBER ONE:
Toss together:

Texas Goat Cheese
Marinated artichoke hearts
Chives, snipped

Tarragon
Cold, boiled pasta with a
vinaigrette dressing.

SALAD NUMBER TWO:
Toss together:

Ancho Chile Cheese
Celery, sliced or chunked
Onion, diced
Pimento, diced
Capers

Black olives
Green pepper, diced
Cold, boiled rice with a
vinaigrette dressing.

Submitted by The Mozzarella Company

SUGGESTED USES FOR Mr. Bar-B-Q Seasonings and Sauces

• Barbeque Sauce—Let simmer ½ hour before serving for a thick, rich, natural flavor.
• All-Purpose Seasoning—Use for seasoning meats before cooking indoors or out. For an extra treat, try sprinkling over cooked vegetables; excellent on fresh salads.
• Fajita Marinade and Fajita Seasoning—Flavor your fajitas like the professionals.
• Mesquite Liquid Smoke—Try using this product when your are cooking in your wok.
• Mesquite Flavored Steak Sauce—Delicious on any prepared steak or hamburger. Adds that great mesquite flavor.

Submitted by Mr. Bar-B-Q Inc.

WHITE CHOCOLATE MACADAMEROON PARFAIT

Ice cream, vanilla or coconut
Neal's White Chocolate
   Madadameroon cookies
Flaked coconut

Macadamia nuts, roughly
   chopped
Coconut liquer (optional)

Roughly crush cookies. Soften ice cream slightly. Layer in parfait glasses (or tall goblets) some cookies, ice cream, coconut, macadamia nuts and liquer if desired. Either serve immediately or return glasses to freezer and allow to freeze solidly, but remove from freezer 20 minutes before serving.

Submitted by Editor for Neal's Cookies

PACE FAJITAS

1½ lbs. beek skirt steaks
1 cup PACE Picante Sauce
¼ cup vegetable oil
1 tsp. lemon juice
Dash of pepper

Dash of garlic powder
Chunky Guacamole
12 flour tortillas (8 to 10 inch),
　heated

Pound meat with meat mallet to tenderize. Place in plastic bag. Combine picante sauce, oil, lemon juice, pepper and garlic powder. Pour into bag and fasten securely. Refrigerate 3 to 24 hours, turning several times. Drain meat, reserving marinade. Place meat on grill over hot coals or on rack of broiler pan. Cook 5 to 6 minutes on each side or until well done, basting frequently with reserved marinade. Remove from grill. Slice across grain into thin strips. Place meat on tortillas. Top with Chunky Guacamole and additional picante sauce. Roll up. Makes 6 servings.

VARIATIONS: Substitute top round steak cut ½ to ¾ inch thick or flank steak for skirt steak. Substitute 1½ lbs. pork steaks or tenderloin cut ½ to ¾ inch thick for skirt steaks. Grill or broil 15 minutes, basting with marinade. Turn and continue cooking 7 to 10 minutes or until well done, basting frequently. Substitute 1½ lbs. boned and skinned chicken breasts for skirt steaks. Grill or broil 8 minutes, basting with marinade. Turn and continue cooking 5 to 7 minutes or until cooked through, basting frequently.

Submitted by Pace Foods Inc.

CHUNKY GUACAMOLE

2 ripe avocados, peeled, seeded
　and diced
1 medium tomato, seeded and
　chopped

⅓ cup green onion slices or
　chopped onion
¼ cup PACE Picante Sauce
1 tsp. lemon juice
¼ tsp. salt

Combine all ingredients, mixing lightly. Chill. Makes about 2½ cups.

Submitted by Pace Foods Inc.

PACE BLOODY MARIA

3 cups tomato juice, chilled
⅓ cup PACE Picante Sauce
2 to 3 T. lemon juice

2 T. Worcestershire sauce
1 tsp. celery salt
1 cup vodka

Combine 1 cup tomato juice, picante sauce, lemon juice, Worcestershire sauce and celery salt in blender container. Blend until smooth. Add remaining tomato juice and vodka. Blend at low speed. Serve over ice, garnished with lemon slice. Makes 5¼ cups, about 6 servings.

Submitted by Pace Foods Inc.

CREMA DE SALSA SOUP

2 cups chopped onion
2 cloves garlic, minced
3 T. butter or oleo
1½ cups PACE Picante Sauce

1 tsp. ground cumin
Dash of ground white pepper
1 quart half and half
Shredded Cheddar cheese

Cook onion and garlic in butter in Dutch oven over medium heat, stirring ocasionally, until onion is tender but not brown. Stir in picante sauce, cumin and pepper. Heat through but do not boil. Gradually stir in half and half. Heat through but do not boil. Ladle soup into individual bowls. Top generously with cheese. Makes 6 to 8 servings, about 7 cups of soup.

Submitted by Pace Foods Inc.

PAPE'S PECAN PIE

3 eggs, lightly beaten
¼ stick of butter
½ cup brown sugar
⅛ tsp. salt

1 cup white corn syrup
1 tsp. vanilla
2 cups chopped pecans

Mix ingredients as listed. Mix well, but by hand. Pour into a 9 inch pie shell. Bake 5 minutes at 350°, then reduce heat to 325° and bake for 35 minutes or until knife comes out clean. Let cool and serve.

Submitted by Pape's Pecan House

SMOOTH AND CRUNCHY SPINACH CASSEROLE

2 pkgs. (10 oz. ea.) frozen chopped
     spinach
1 (3 oz.) pkg. cream cheese
¼ cup butter

¼ cup grated Parmesan cheese
½ cup chopped pecans
Salt and pepper to taste

Preheat oven to 350°. Cook spinach in salted water. Drain. Melt cream cheese and butter together. Add to spinach. Salt and pepper to taste. Pour into buttered casserole dish. Top with Parmesan cheese and pecans. Bake until bubbly, about 30 minutes. Serves 6 to 8.

Submitted by Pecan Valley Nut Company Inc.

PECAN BROCCOLI

2 lbs. broccoli
Salt
Black pepper
Fresh lemon juice

⅓ cup pecans
4 T. unsalted butter
1 finely chopped garlic clove

Remove and discard large leaves and tough portions of stem from broccoli. Wash broccoli, drain and tie securely into bunches with cotton string. Cook, tightly covered, in small amount of water 15 to 30 minutes or until tender. Drain. Remove string. Arrange broccoli on warm platter. Season with salt, pepper and sprinkle with lemon juice. Saute pecans in butter until lightly brown. Add garlic. Sprinkle garlic butter and pecans over broccoli. Serve at once. Serves 6.

Submitted by Pecan Valley Nut Company Inc.

ORANGE PECANDY

2 cups sugar
⅛ tsp. salt
4 T. corn syrup
¾ cup evaporated milk
Juice of 1 orange

1 tsp. grated orange peel
¼ cup butter
1 tsp. vanilla
1 cup lightly toasted pecans

Bring sugar, salt, syrup and milk to boil. Add orange juice and cook to 234° on candy thermometer. Add peel. Cook to 250°. Cool. Add butter, vanilla and nuts. Beat. Drop by teaspoonfuls onto greased cookie sheet. Store in airtight container.

Submitted by Pecan Valley Nut Company Inc.

NUTTY NOODLES

1 pkg (8 oz.) egg noodles
Salt
¼ cup bread crumbs
½ cup chopped pecans

6 T. melted butter, divided
1 T. dry sherry
2 T. parsley
¼ cup Parmesan cheese

Cook noodles in boiling, salted water. Drain. Meanwhile, in a skillet, toss bread crumbs and pecans with 3 tablespoons butter. Saute over medium heat until lightly toasted. Toss noodles with remaining butter, sherry, parsley and salt to taste. Put in a 2 quart casserole. Cover with Parmesan cheese, crumbs and pecans. Serve at once or keep warm in 250° oven 5 to 10 minutes. Serves 6.

Submitted by Pecan Valley Nut Company Inc.

PECAN CHEESE CRISPS

½ cup butter
8 oz. grated Cheddar cheese
1 T. Worcestershire sauce
1¼ cup flour

½ tsp. salt
⅛ tsp. red pepper
⅛ tsp. Tabasco sauce
1 cup finely chopped pecans

Cream butter and cheese and add remaining ingredients. Chill dough until firm enough to form into rolls 1 inch thick. Place rolls in freezer (may be stored indefinitely). Defrost 10 minutes and slice into thin rounds. Place on ungreased cookie sheet and bake about 10 minutes at 350°. Makes 4 to 5 dozen.

Submitted by Pecan Valley Nut Company Inc.

PECAN VEGETABLE SALAD

3 cups leaf or iceberg lettuce
Salt, pepper, sugar
1½ cups shredded Swiss cheese
1 pkg. (10 oz.) thawed frozen peas
4 sliced hard boiled eggs

¾ cup broken pecans
½ medium head Romaine lettuce
   OR 1½ cups spinach
¾ cup salad dressing or
   mayonnaise

Place lettuce in bottom of a large bowl. Sprinkle with a little salt, pepper and sugar. Top with the cheese. Spoon peas on top of cheese spreading evenly. Arrange egg slices and pecans over peas. Sprinkle eggs with salt. Remove heavy midrib of Romaine or spinach then tear into bite size pieces. Arrange on top of eggs and pecans. Spread salad dressing or mayonnaise on top, sealing to edge of bowl. Cover and chill the salad in refrigerator for 24 hours or overnight. Toss before serving. Serves 10 to 12.

Submitted by Pecan Valley Nut Company Inc.

PECAN BAKED FISH

¾ cup dry whole wheat bread crumbs	½ tsp. onion powder
½ cup pecans	½ tsp. salt
¼ cup toasted wheat germ	¼ tsp. pepper
½ tsp. thyme leaves	1½ lb. fish fillets
½ tsp. garlic powder	1 beaten egg

Dry bread crumbs (made from 1½ slices whole wheat bread) briefly in the oven. Grind pecans until fine in blender, food processor or hand grater. Mix together breadcrumbs, pecans, wheat germ, thyme, garlic and onion powders, salt and pepper. Dip fillets in egg and then in crumb mixture. Place on lightly oiled rack in shallow baking pan. Preheat oven to 450°. Bake 10 minutes for each inch of thickness of the fillet at its thickest part, turning once. Fish should flake easily with a fork when done. Serves 6 at 215 calories per serving.

Submitted by Pecan Valley Nut Company Inc.

PERFECT BISCUITS

3 cups Pioneer Biscuit and Baking Mix	1 cup milk

Preheat oven to 450°. Lightly grease a baking pan. Blend Pioneer Biscuit and Baking Mix with milk, stirring well. Turn onto board sprinkled with Pioneer Biscuit and Baking Mix and form dough into a ball. Knead 2 or 3 times. Roll or pat to ½ inch thickness. Cut with sharp 2 inch cutter without twisting. Place close together on a prepared baking sheet. Bake 11 to 13 minutes. Brush tops with melted butter or margarine when biscuits come out of oven. For drop biscuits: after blending, drop by spoonfuls on prepared baking sheet. Yields 18 biscuits.

Submitted by Pioneer Flour Mills

LIME GRILLED CHICKEN

Juice of 3 large limes
Grate the peels of 2 limes
¼ cup olive oil
1 tsp. thyme
1 tsp. rosemary

¼ tsp. cayenne pepper
4 cloves garlic, pressed
2 tsps. Worcestershire
1 tsp. prepared mustard
3 T. soy sauce

Cut chicken in halves or quarters and marinate for 4 hours or overnight in the refrigerator. Grill until done over 100% mesquite charcoal for best results. Can also be grilled over gas or briquets.

Submitted by Primarily Barbecue

MESQUITE HERB GRILLED FISH AND SEAFOOD

Brush fish, shrimp or other seafood with olive oil or a good grade of vegetable oil. Season lightly with garlic powder, black pepper to taste, a touch of salt if desired. The majority of flavor will come from the Primarily Barbecue Mesquite Herb Mix. Wet the mesquite herb mix, and let soak while starting fire of Primarily Barbecue's 100% Mesquite Lump Charcoal. When coals are of desired heat level, sprinkle with the wet mesquite herb mix and grill as usual. While wet method of grilling is recommended — for slow release of smoke — some of the finer herbs are lost in the water. Therefore, an alternate method is to sprinkle DRY mesquite herb mix over hot coals. This method gives quick release of smoke and seasoning. It requires the use of more mix, but also imparts more flavor, particularly for quick cooking items such as fish and seafood.

EDITOR'S NOTE: The product called for in the above recipe, i.e. Mesquite Herb Mix, is an unusual (if not unique) combination of tiny mesquite chips and various herbs. Some of these herbs, which are visually identifiable, include bay leaf, rosemary and thyme. The mix, however, incorporates other herbs which produce a particularly savory and permeating taste. Yet, one which is still subtle and tantalizing. Our editorial recommended uses are also for chicken and lamb. Presumably it could be used on any meat — beef, pork or goat. Or turkey. Or any wild game.

Submitted by Primarily Barbecue

INFORMATION ON CHARCOAL FOR GRILLING OR BARBECUE

Preposterous as it may seem — because there were more than 125 million barbecue grills in service in 1985 — the fact remains that few enough people know much about the process, and even less about the fuel they use.

Nevertheless, whether a person is doing a simple grilling operation — of hot dogs, hamburgers or steaks — or the long, hot and often tedious work of pit barbecue, one of the prime ingredients in the affair is the fuel.

The fuel can be charcoal or wood — and what kind of either is an important factor in the ultimate taste outcome.

As to wood, experts all disagree. Some prefer hickory, some oak, some mesquite. Some fastidious and discriminatory cooks choose different woods for different recipes, using pecan for this dish, peach or mulberry for another, and still other types of hardwoods or fruitwoods for the whole range of their cooking repertory.

But regardless of the wood used, all agree on one thing. The wood must be allowed to burn down to glowing coals before the meat, fowl or fish can be put atop the fire.

As for charcoal, the same kind of choosiness exists among the serious cooks. They demand real lump charcoal — not briquets.

Briquets were invented by Henry Ford in the 1920s as a means of disposing of byproducts from one of his factories. And they were originally used as fuel for industrial plants.

Today, most briquets are still made from industrial waste products with some cornstarch included to bind the material and sodium nitrate or other chemicals added to help them burn better. For serious cooks, the chemical taste that is thus transferred to the food is offensive in the extreme.

It would, therefore, behoove consumers to read the contents on labels of any charcoal briquets they buy.

The important wording is 100% pure charcoal. Otherwise, use wood.

Wood chips and wood chunks on gas or electric grills will provide some of the taste qualities of the appropriately flavored charcoal.

Editor

FIDEO PRONTO

1 pkg.(15 oz.) Q & Q Vermicelli
1 can (16 oz.) seasoned stewed tomatoes, chopped

1 tsp. sugar
3 T. cooking oil or bacon drippings

Heat oil or bacon drippings in heavy skillet. Add uncooked vermicelli and saute over medium flame, stirring constantly, until golden brown. Add tomatoes and sugar, cover, and steam for about eight minutes or until vermicelli is "bitey"—tender but still slightly firm. Salt and pepper to taste, sprinkle with grated Parmesan if desired. Serves five—delicious side dish with meats or fowl. FOR SPICY VARIETY: Add 1 medium onion and 1 small green bell pepper. Chop, saute with vermicelli and proceed as above. Either seasoned or plain canned tomatoes may be used for this variation.

Submitted by Q & Q Brand, Fort Worth Macaroni Co.

CHEESE NACHO DIP

1 can Ricos Nacho Cheese Sauce
½ pint sour cream
1 jar (8 oz.) Ricos Picante Sauce

1 small onion, finely chopped
Garlic powder, to taste

Blend all ingredients until smooth. Garnish with pimentos, bacon bits or green onion tops, or add an extra spicy touch by sprinkling with Ricos Jalapeno Peppers.

Submitted by Ricos

RYE CANAPE WEDGES

Trim bottom crust from a round loaf of rye bread. Cut in layers ½ inch thick. Alternate layers with Ricos Cheese Nacho Dip and deviled ham. Top with apple slices. Chill until serving time. Cut in wedges and serve.

Submitted by Ricos

SAUSAGE SNACK BISCUITS

3 cups Bisquick
1 can Ricos Nacho Cheese Sauce

1 egg
1 lb. Owen sausage

Mix all together. Roll out on floured board ½ inch thick. Cut with cookie cutter. Place in shallow pan which has been sprayed with Pam. Bake at 350° until brown, about 30 minutes. This is hard to mix and hard to cut, but very good. Makes several biscuits. Good served with eggs or hash brown potatoes or as a snack.

Submitted by Ricos

CHEESE DEVILED EGGS

1 dozen eggs, boiled, sliced in half
Mayonnaise and vinegar to taste

⅓ can Ricos Aged Cheddar
Cheese Sauce

Remove yolks from egg whites, mash. Add vinegar and mayonnaise to taste, mix well. Add Ricos Aged Cheddar Cheese Sauce. Mix thoroughly. Spoon into egg white halves. Sprinkle with paprika or bacon bits or chopped green onion tops.

Submitted by Ricos

STUFFED JALAPENOS

1 can Ricos Jalapeno Peppers and
    Stems, choose largest
1 lb. ground meat
1 medium onion, chopped

1 quart buttermilk
2 cups flour
Seasoned salt and pepper to taste
Garlic powder to taste

Leave stems on peppers. Make small slit in whole jalapeno peppers, remove all seed and veins. Rinse with cold water. Soak peppers in buttermilk for 1 hour. Reserve buttermilk. Brown ground meat, onion, pepper, garlic powder and seasoned salt in skillet. Stuff peppers with meat mixture. Dip in buttermilk, roll in a mixture of flour, salt and pepper. Dip and roll again. Fry in deep fat until golden brown.

NOTE: Peppers may also be stuffed with cheddar cheese, boiled eggs or shrimp.

Submitted by Ricos

NACHO CHEESE POTATO DISH

5 medium potatoes, peeled and
  sliced in round slices
1 medium onion, chopped
1 can onion soup
1 tsp. parsley flakes

1 can Ricos Nacho Cheese Sauce
Dash of salt and black pepper
4 slices fried crisp bacon,
  crumbled
1 cup celery, chopped

Mix with can of soup the parsley, pepper and salt. Pour over potatoes which have been combined with onion and celery. Pour cheese on top, sprinkle with bacon bits and bake about 1 hour at 350° or until potatoes are done.

Submitted by Ricos

EGGPLANT CASSEROLE

1 large eggplant, cubed and boiled
  til tender
¼ tsp. pepper
1 can mushroom soup
2 tsp. chopped green onions

1 medium size package snack
  cracker, crushed
4 slices crisp bacon, crumbled
½ can Ricos Nacho Cheese Sauce

Drain eggplant, add pepper, green onions, bacon. Add half the cracker crumbs. Mix mushroom soup and cheese sauce. Pour over eggplant mixture. Top with remaining cracker crumbs. Bake 25 minutes at 375°.

Submitted by Ricos

SQUASH 'N CHEESE

About 2 lbs. yellow squash, sliced
1 large onion, peeled and sliced
1 stick butter or margarine

Salt and pepper to taste
2 cups cracker crumbs
½ can Ricos Nacho Cheese Sauce

Cook squash and onions in small amount of water until tender. Add butter, salt and pepper, 1 cup cracker crumbs, ½ can cheese sauce. Pour into baking dish which has been buttered well. Sprinkle with remaining cup of cracker crumbs. Sprinkle with paprika.

Submitted by Ricos

MACARONI or RICE 'N CHEESE

6 cups cooked macaroni or rice
1 can Ricos Nacho Cheese Sauce

Bread crumbs
Paprika

Stir cheese into macaroni or rice. Garnish with bread crumbs and paprika. Bake 30 minutes at 350° or til bubbly. NOTE: Add diced ham or sausage for one dish dinner.

Submitted by Ricos

CHEESE VEGETABLE SOUP

¼ cup butter
½ cup minced onion
½ cup flour
¼ tsp. baking soda
1½ tsp. salt
¼ tsp. paprika

2½ cups milk
2 cups boullion
½ cup diced carrots
½ cup diced celery
1 cup Ricos Nacho Cheese Sauce
1 T. chopped parsley

In a large saucepan, melt butter. Saute onion lightly. Add flour, baking soda and seasonings. Blend well. Slowly add milk and boullion to mixture, stirring constantly to make a smooth white sauce. Add vegetables and cheese sauce. Simmer 15 minutes or until vegetables are tender. DO NOT BOIL. (Soup may curdle.) Serve topped with parsley.

Submitted by Ricos

ASPARAGUS WITH RAREBIT SAUCE

¼ cup butter
¼ cup flour
1 tsp. white pepper
⅓ tsp. dry mustard
4 cups cooked rice

1 cup milk
½ can Ricos Cheese Sauce
2 lbs. fresh asparagus, cooked
8 slices crisp bacon

Melt butter in large saucepan, stir in flour, salt, pepper and dry mustard. Slowly add milk to mixture and cook over low heat, stirring constantly until mixture is thick and smooth. Blend in cheese sauce and remove from heat. Arrange asparagus on rice, pour on rarebit sauce and top with bacon strips. NOTE: Rarebit sauce may be used over broccoli, cauliflower, brussel sprouts, potatoes, baked or steamed onions and meat dishes.

Submitted by Ricos

CHICKEN SPAGHETTI SUPREME

2 chickens, about 4 lbs. each
2 onions, quartered
1 large carrot, cut in 1 inch
    lengths
2 ribs of celery plus leaves
10 peppercorns
3 sprigs of parsley
2 cans tomatoes, chopped
2 cups green pepper, chopped
3 cups onion, finely chopped
1½ sticks butter
1 bay leaf
2 cups celery, finely chopped

6 cloves garlic, minced
1 lb. mushrooms, thinly sliced
1 lb. round steak, ground
¼ tsp. thyme
1 cup flour
6 cups chicken stock
½ cup whipping cream
2 lbs. vermicelli
Salt and pepper
1 can (17 oz.) Ricos Aged Cheddar
    Cheese Sauce
2 cups Parmesan cheese, grated

Place chickens in deep kettle. Add quartered onions, carrot pieces, celery ribs and leaves, parsley, peppercorns, and salt to taste. Add cold water just to cover, bring to a boil, reduce heat and simmer until tender. Allow chicken to remain in stock until ready to use. Place tomatoes in a large kettle. In skillet, saute mushrooms, celery, onion, green pepper and garlic in ½ stick of butter until onions are translucent. Add to tomatoes. Brown ground round in same skillet with bay leaf, thyme, salt and pepper to taste. Add to tomatoes and simmer for 20 to 30 minutes, stirring from the bottom occasionally. Melt 1 stick butter in saucepan, add flour and stir with wire whisk, Add stock, stirring til thickened. Stir in cream and combine with tomato mixture. Remove skin from chicken and cut into large bite sized pieces. Cook vermicelli al dente. Rinse well. Place a little sauce in the bottom of a casserole dish. Add a layer of vermicelli, then chicken, cheese sauce and more sauce. Continue to layer. Sprinkle with grated parmesan cheese. Bake uncovered at 400° till heated. (This recipe serves 16 and is excellent for parties.)

Submitted by Ricos

CHICKEN CHEESE ROLLS

4 split boned, skinned, chicken breasts	4 slices bacon
	1 can Ricos Aged Cheddar Cheese
4 oz. cream cheese	Sauce
Chopped chives	½ cup Ricos Picante Sauce
Garlic salt	

On waxed paper pound chicken until about ½ inch thick. Spread 1 T. cream cheese onto each breast. Sprinkle with chives and garlic salt. Roll up. Wrap with bacon and secure with toothpick. Place in shallow baking dish, cover with cheese sauce, then picante sauce. Bake at 375° for 45 minutes. Let set 15 minutes before serving. Serves 4.

Submitted by Ricos

CHICKEN CHEESE RICE

3 cups diced, cooked chicken	1 small onion, finely diced
3 cups cooked rice	Salt and pepper
1 can Ricos Aged Cheddar Cheese	Bread crumbs
Sauce	Paprika

Mix cheese sauce with cooked rice and chopped onion. Spread one half of the mixture in a casserole, add diced chicken on top, cover with remaining cheese rice, top with bread crumbs and sprinkle with paprika. Bake for 20 minutes in a moderate oven. NOTE: Try topping with Ricos Picante Sauce instead of paprika for a special taste.

Submitted by Ricos

SALMON CHEESE LOAF

1 large can red salmon
½ cup green onions
½ cup finely chopped green
　peppers
¼ tsp. black pepper

1 small can evaporated milk
1 cup bread crumbs (wheat bread
　is best)
2 eggs
1 can Ricos Nacho Cheese Sauce

Mix all ingredients together except cheese sauce. Put in a loaf pan that has been sprayed with Pam. Pour cheese sauce over top of loaf. Cover and bake 45 minutes at 350°.

Submitted by Ricos

TUNA BEAN BAKE

1 large can tuna, flaked
2 cups macaroni, cooked
2 cans sliced green beans
1 can celery soup

1 can small whole potatoes
1 can (6 oz.) fried onions
1 cup milk
1 can Ricos Nacho Cheese Sauce

Put macaroni in bottom of baking dish, sprinkle with half the tuna, 1 can green beans, ½ can onions, 1 can potatoes. Repeat layers with remaining ingredients, except onions. Mix milk with the cheese sauce and pour over the layers. Sprinkle with remaining onions. Bake 30 minutes.

Submitted by Ricos

TUNA TETRAZZINI

4 cups cooked macaroni
1 small can tuna, drained
1 small can mushrooms or ½ cup
　fresh mushrooms
1 large green pepper, chopped
1 medium onion, chopped

1 small jar pimentos
1 cup milk
1 cup cracker crumbs
1 can Ricos Nacho Cheese Sauce
Black pepper, optional

Combine macaroni, tuna, onions, green peppers, pimentos and mushrooms and toss lightly. Pour into casserole dish. Stir milk and cheese sauce till creamy, pour over tuna mixture. Sprinkle top with cracker crumbs. Bake at 350° for 25 minutes.

Submitted by Ricos

COMPANY SEAFOOD

2 lbs. fish fillets	1½ cups cashew nuts
white wine	Capers
1 can (17 oz.) Ricos Aged Cheddar Cheese Sauce	

Poach fish in wine. Remove from wine and place in shallow baking dish. Cover with cheese sauce. Sprinkle with cashews and capers. Bake in moderate oven for 15 to 20 minutes. Serve with wild rice. A real gourmet meal that is so easy to make.

Submitted by Ricos

CHEESE BAKED SNAPPER

1 red snapper, about 3 lbs.	½ can Ricos Cheese Sauce
1 can (8 oz.) evaporated milk	Capers

Have a 3 lb. snapper prepared for baking, leaving head on fish. Place in a buttered baking dish. Pour the milk over the fish and bake at 350° for 30 minutes. Pour heated cheese over fish. Sprinkle with capers and bake another 15 minutes. Serves 4 to 5.

Submitted by Ricos

FONDUE FRUIT

Orange slices	Pear slices
Apple slices	Strawberries
Pineapple chunks	Ricos Aged Cheddar Cheese Sauce

Peel and slice or chunk fruit. Heat cheese sauce in a double boiler or fondue pot. Using long toothpicks or fondue forks or long skewers, Dip fruit in warmed cheese. Good as a dessert or appetizer.

Submitted by Ricos

TEXAS WINE JELLIES

The following jellies are made from Llano Estacado Wine:

Chenin Blanc Johannisberg	Llano Red
Riesling	Rose of Cabernet
French Colombard	Hot Pepper Wine
Llano Blush	Mild Pepper Wine

SUGGESTED USES:

• Use Pepper Wine jellies on crackers topped with cream cheese. Also use as a marinade for wild game or a glaze for outdoor grilling.

Other Wine Jellies can be used as follows:
• Serve on graham crackers topped with cream cheese.
• Use in place of cranberry sauce at Thanksgiving.

- Serve as an accompaniment to steaks, roasts and other meats.
- Use with wheat crackers as an hors d'oeuvre at your next wine tasting.
- Good with peanut butter on homemade bread.
- Spread on warm cake fresh from the oven.
- For a wine flavored icing, put 3 or 4 T. of the wine jelly into your 7 minute frosting while cooking.
- Serve at breakfast with buttered toast, hot biscuits, English muffins, bagels or any other type of bread.

Submitted by Roaring Springs Jam Factory

TEXAS SPRITZER

Into a glass, pour over ice:

⅓ cup cranberry or cranapple juice	**⅔ cup Rosser Vasser**
	Squeeze of lime (optional)

Editor's note: Rosser Vasser is a Texas Sparkling Water, which has a taste quite unlike regular club soda. Any fruit juice may be substituted in the above recipe, for a delightful non-alcoholic drink.

Submitted by Rosser Vasser

BLUEBERRY JELLY FILLED MUFFINS

2 cups all purpose flour	**1 egg, slightly beaten**
¼ cup sugar	**1 cup milk**
1 T. baking powder	**¼ cup melted butter or margarine**
½ tsp. Salt	**Blueberry jelly (or any jelly)**

Combine dry ingredients in large mixing bowl. Combine milk, egg and butter. Mix well. Make a hole in center of dry ingredients. Pour in liquid and mix until JUST moistened. Fill greased muffin pans ¼ full. Spoon 1 tsp. blueberry jelly in center of each muffin cup. Add remaining batter over jelly, filling each cup half full. Bake at 400° for 20 to 25 minutes. Remove muffins immediately from pans to cool.

Submitted by Mary Smith, Sandy Foot Farm

BLUEBERRY BUTTERMILK MUFFINS

2 cups all purpose flour	**1 egg, beaten slightly**
½ cup sugar	**1 cup buttermilk**
2¼ tsp. baking powder	**¼ cup melted butter or margarine**
1 tsp. salt	**1 cup blueberries**
¼ tsp. soda	

Combine dry ingredients in a mixing bowl. Set aside. Combine egg, buttermilk, and butter. Mix well. Make a hole in center of dry ingredients. Pour in the liquid ingredients. Stir until JUST moistened. Fold in blueberries. Fill greased muffin pans two-thirds full. Bake in 425° oven 20 to 25 minutes. When done, remove from pan immediately. Makes 1½ dozen muffins.

Submitted by Mary Smith, Sandy Foot Farm

BLUEBERRY ICE CREAM

2 cups blueberries
1 cup sugar, divided
1 T. fresh lemon juice
1 tsp. grated lemon peel

5 egg yolks at room temperature
2 cups milk, scalded
2 cups whipping cream

Sort blueberries. Crush slightly in bowl. Toss with ½ cup sugar, lemon juice and peel. Refrigerate for 12 hours. Next day (or later same day), scald milk. Beat yolks in large bowl of electric mixer. Add remaining ½ cup sugar and beat until mixture is pale yellow and slowly dissolving ribbon forms when beaters are lifted (about 6 minutes.) Slowly beat in hot milk. Pour mixture into heavy large saucepan and cook over medium or low heat, stirring constantly until custard is 180° and leaves a path of back of spoon when finger is drawn across it. DO NOT BOIL. Stir in berries. Blend in cream. Cool. Refrigerate until chilled. Transfer blueberry mixture to ice cream freezer and process according to instructions. Turn into plastic container. Cover and freeze. Soften in refrigerator before serving — at least 15 minutes. Makes 8 servings.

Submitted by Mary Smith, Sandy Foot Farm

NOONDAY ONIONS

10 Noonday sweet onions
2 dozen ice cubes

Assorted dips, if you like

Peel and trim onions to your preference. We find it awfully handy to have about 6 or 8 inches of the tops available for a handle and just nibblin' on as well. Place ice cubes in a large bowl — one you like a lot. (It makes for a nice setting.) Fill the bowl ¾ full of water and add trimmed onions. Let sit for 10 minutes or so. Dip cool, sweet onion in your favorite dip and enjoy. (They are great just plain, too.)

Submitted by Sandy Hill Farm

SPICY HUSHPUPPIES

1 cup Jalapeno Cornbread Mix
¼ tsp. garlic salt

1 egg
¼ cup milk

Oil or shortening for deep frying. Preheat oil or shortening to 350. to 375°. Mix dry ingredients. Add egg and milk. Stir until blended. Drop by teaspoonful into hot oil or shortening. Cook 3 to 4 minutes until golden brown.

NOTE: A melon ball scooper or small ice cream scoop works well to shape hushpuppies. Yields 18 hushpuppies (1½ inch size)

Submitted by San Antonio River Mill

MEXICAN STYLE CHICKEN AND FISH BREADING

1¼ cups Jalapeno Cornbread Mix   ¼ cup milk
1 egg

Mix egg and milk in a shallow dish. Pour Jalapeno Cornbread Mix onto a plate. Dip chicken or fish in egg and milk mixture. Roll in cornbread mix to coat. Fry or bake chicken or fish as desired. NOTE: This recipe coats approximately 3½ lbs. of chicken or fish pieces.

Submitted by San Antonio River Mill

SUGGESTED USED FOR JALAPENO JELLIES

• For snacks and cocktails — cream cheese and a dab of jalapeno jelly on crackers.
• As a "gringo nacho"— jalapeno jelly with cheese and corn chips.
• "Texas Cranberry Sauce"— on meat, poultry, wild game.
• Bring new life to a fluffy cheese omelet.
• "Grilled Cheese International"— spread jalapeno jelly on cheese before heating.
• For a refreshing dessert — on vanilla ice cream.
• As a glaze for pork roast or ham.

Submitted by Serendipity of the Valley

SHINER RED HORSERADISH

1 large horseradish root   1 bottle Shiner Beer
1 fresh red beet

Peel and grate the horseradish into a medium size bowl. Peel and grate the beet into the same bowl. Add enough Shiner beer to moisten to desired consistency. Serve as a spread on cold cuts, in cocktail sauce or with roasted meats.

Submitted by Christine Lease for Shiner Beer

SHINER BATTER FOR DEEP FRYING

1⅓ cups flour   1 T. melted butter
1 tsp. salt   2 beaten egg yolks; reserve whites
½ tsp. white pepper   ¾ cup flat Shiner Beer

Combine flour, salt, pepper, butter and egg yolks. Mix well. Gradually add Shiner beer, stirring constantly. Refrigerate at least 3 hours. Just before using, beat egg whites until stiff and fold into mixture. NOTE: This batter is especially good for dipping mushrooms, zucchini, cauliflower, shrimp, lobster, or catfish before deep frying.

Submitted by Christine Lease for Shiner Beer

SHINER-ING ROAST

4 to 5 Lb. beef roast
1 jar (16 oz.) Dickie Davis Sweet
   and Hot Sauce

1 bottle Shiner Bock Beer
3 T. oil
Pepper to taste

Preheat oven to 350°. Put oil in roasting pan on top of stove at high heat. Add roast and sear both sides until browned. Remove from heat. Sprinkle top of roast with pepper as desired, then pour Dickie Davis Sweet and Hot Sauce and Shiner Bock Beer on top. Cover and bake 2½ to 3 hours or until tender. Serves 8 to 10.

Submitted by Christine Lease for Shiner Beer

STRAWBERRY PUDDING

5 T. butter, softened
1 cup flour
1½ tsps. baking powder
½ tsp. ground cinnamon
¼ tsp. salt
⅔ cup sugar

2 eggs, slightly beaten
½ cup buttermilk
1 tsp. finely grated orange peel
1 tsp. orange extract
1 jar Soupcon's Strawberry
   Amaretto Sauce

Preheat oven to 350°. Coat bottom and sides of 9 by 5 by 3 loaf pan with 1 tablespoon of softened butter. Sift flour, baking powder, cinnamon and salt into a small bowl and set aside. In a large mixing bowl, cream the remaining 4 tablespoons of butter and sugar together until light and fluffy. Beat in the eggs. Beat in the flour mixture ¼ cup at a time, moistening the mixture after each addition with a little of the buttermilk. Continue this process until all the ingredients are combined and the batter is smooth. Add the orange peel and almond extract. Spread the jar of Strawberry Amaretto Sauce into the bottom of the buttered loaf pan. Pour the batter on top of the preserves and bake in the middle of the oven for 40 to 50 minutes. Cool the pudding in the pan for about 10 minutes. With a long knife, run around the inside edges of pan. Place an inverted serving plate over the pan and quickly turn them over. Pudding should slide out easily. Serve warm. Serves 4 to 6.

Submitted by Soupcon Corporation

STRAWBERRY AMARETTO DESSERT

1½ cups crushed vanilla wafers
⅓ cup melted butter
⅔ cup toasted slivered almonds
1 tsp. almond extract

½ gallon vanilla ice cream
1 jar (10 oz.) Soupcon's
   Strawberry Amaretto Sauce

Combine vanilla wafers, butter, almonds and almond extract. Spread half of the mixture into a 9 inch square pan. Pat firmly. Reserve remainder for topping. Soften ice cream and spoon over crumb mixture in pan. Place pan in freezer to firm, about 20 minutes. Remove pan from freezer and quickly spread Strawberry Amaretto Sauce over ice cream.

Sprinkle with remaining crumbs. Cover pan and freeze. Remove pan from freezer 20 minutes before serving. Cut into 9 squares.

Submitted by Soupcon Corporation

POACHED PEARS WITH FRUIT COMPOTE

4 Comice, Bartlett or Bosc pears,
ripe but firm
1 bottle (12 oz.) Soupcon's
Cr-Razz-Berry Dazzle Syrup

Zest of one lemon
1 jar Soupcon Fudge Sauce,
warmed slightly

Peel and core pears, cutting into halves. In a saucepan, combine syrup and lemon zest and bring to a boil. Reduce heat to simmer and add pears. The poaching liquid should completely cover the pears while cooking. Add water or red wine to cover if needed. Cook pears until tender. Leave in liquid until ready to serve. At serving time, place pears on a dessert plate and spoon fudge sauce into cavity of each pear half. Drizzle with remaining poaching liquid. Serves 4.

Submitted by Soupcon Corporation

FAJITAS
(Beef Skirt Steaks)

Use 2 lbs. beef skirt steaks (or flank steak) to serve 4 to 5 persons. Trim excess fat from meat. Squeeze fresh lime juice over both sides and sprinkle liberally with MENCHACA BRAND Fajita Seasoning. Let stand 15 to 30 minutes (or overnight in refrigerator for maximum tenderness. Sear the meat on both sides over hot charcoal or mesquite wood fire to seal in juices. Allow to cook until done to your satisfaction. The meat will be most tender if not over-cooked. Slice the meat across the grain and serve in folded, hot, flour tortillas. Garnish with guacamole and pico de gallo (a mixture of chopped tomato, onion, fresh jalapeno and cilantro to taste.) Other garnish suggestions include picante sauce and sour cream.

Submitted by South Texas Spice Company

FAJITA MARINADE

¾ cup oil
1 cup white vinegar
¼ cup soy sauce
1 cup water

¼ cup lemon juice
½ tsp. ground black pepper
3 or 4 T. Menchaca Brand Fajita
Seasoning

Mix above ingredients well. Marinate 5 to 6 lbs. of meat in refrigerator overnight. Also good as marinade for fish or chicken.

Submitted by South Texas Spice Company

FAJITA RANCH STYLE PARTY DIP

4 tsps. Menchaca Brand Fajita
Seasoning

1 tsp. crushed parsley flakes
2 cups (one pint) sour cream

Mix well and refrigerate until ready to use.

Submitted by South Texas Spice Company

BARBECUED GOAT

1 yearling goat, cut into
   reasonable serving pieces
   prepared yellow mustard

black pepper
Southwest's Best cooking
   (barbecue) sauce

Mix mustard (use plain hot dog mustard, nothing fancy) and pepper together to make a rather thickish paste. Rub all over goat pieces. Place in flat roasting pan, cover with foil and roast—either in oven or in outdoor roaster—for several hours at VERY LOW heat. Meat should be very tender. Pour Southwest Best over meat pieces. Remove meat pieces from pan and place over grill of mesquite coals. Cook until outside is slightly browned. Baste with additional Southwest Best if needed. Additional Southwest Best may be added to liquid left in roasting pan to make an excellent dipping sauce for barbecued goat.

Submitted by Editor for Southwest's Best

BARBECUED LAMB

1 leg of lamb, butterflied or thick
   lamb chops cut from leg, loin,
   rack or shoulder
Several cloves garlic, chopped
   (optional)

Black pepper (optional)
Southwest's Best cooking
   (barbecue) sauce

Sprinkle cut sides of lamb with garlic and pepper. Set aside and let flavor for a several minutes. Pour Southwest's Best over lamb and let marinate for several hours. Grill lamb or chops over mesquite lump charcoal. Lamb chops may also be pan grilled. The butterflied roast may be roasted in regular oven. Best results, however, obtain from outdoor charcoal cooking.

Submitted by Editor for Southwest's Best

SOUTHWEST'S BEST LAMBURGERS

4 lamb patties, room temperature
4 tsps. butter or margarine or
   olive oil

4 to 6 T. Southwest's Best cooking
   (barbecue) sauce

Put butter, margarine or oil in skillet. Over medium high heat, melt or heat oils and place lamb patties in skillet. Cook 3 to 4 minutes on one side. Turn. Pour Southwest's Best sauce over each of the patties. Let cook another 4 minutes on second side. This will yield rather pink patties. And juicy. For well done meat, increase cooking time. But be careful that sauce does not burn.

Submitted by Editor for Southwest's Best

OLD FASHIONED BUTTERMILK PIE

½ cup butter, softened
2 cups sugar
3 eggs
¼ cup all purpose flour

1 cup Superior buttermilk
Dash of nutmeg
1 unbaked 10-inch pie shell

Combine butter and sugar, cream well. Add eggs and flour. Beat until fluffy (about 2 minutes.) Fold in buttermilk and nutmeg. Pour filling into pastry shell. Bake at 350° for 50 minutes, or until firm.

Submitted by Superior Dairies, Inc.

SERVING SUGGESTIONS FOR HOT AND MILD OKRA PICKLES

• Instead of an olive in a Martini, try an "Okratini."
• Excellent as an accompaniment to hamburgers, hot dogs and barbecue.
• Use as part of a relish plate.
• With tacos or other Mexican food.
• Use as topping on salads.
• Use as an exciting substitute for cucumber pickles.
• Eat right out of the jar.
• As part of a gourmet buffet.
• Slice and place in submarine sandwich.
• Send in ice chests with fishermen on trips.
• Or anytime you want a spicy, crispy, utterly delicious pickle.

Submitted by Talk O' Texas Brands Inc.

CREAMY SALSA DIP

2 pickled jalapenos, diced small
8 oz. cream cheese, softened
¾ cup sour cream

6 oz. Territorial House Green
   Chile Salsa
¼ tsp. salt
Dash pepper

Mix ingredients together in a bowl. Serve chilled with chips or crackers. Makes about 2 cups dip.

Submitted by Territorial House Inc.

GREEN CHILE STEW

4 T. butter or margarine, divided
2 lbs. boneless pork butt
½ tsp. garlic minced
½ tsp. salt
4 potatoes, peeled, chopped in ½
   inch chunks

2 cups water
3 stalks celery, sliced in ½ inch
   pieces
2 cups Territorial House Green
   Chile Salsa

Trim fat from pork, slice into ½ inch cubes. Over medium heat, pan fry meat in 2 Tablespoons butter or margarine with salt and garlic until browned and cooked thoroughly, about 15 minutes. Stir in water and potatoes. Simmer until potatoes are soft, about 15 minutes. Saute celery in remaining butter (or margarine) until soft. Combine celery and salsa with stew. Continue cooking for 10 minutes. Serves 8 to 10.

Submitted by Territorial House Inc.

QUESADILLAS

⅓ cup oil
8 corn tortillas, fried then patted dry with paper towel
16 slices Monterey Jack cheese (1 by 3 inches)
2 small tomatoes cut into 16 thin slices

2 small avocados cut into 16 thin slices
4 oz. sour cream
8 oz. Territorial House Green Chile Salsa
2 cups lettuce, shredded (optional)

Prepare all ingredients before assembling quesadillas. Place 2 tortillas on platter. Top each with 4 cheese slices. Cover with another tortilla. Melt cheese in broiler or oven. Remove. Cut each round into 4 wedges. (A circular pizza cutter works well for cutting.) On each wedge place tomato and avocado slice, 1 Tablespoon chile salsa and 1 dab sour cream. Garnish platter with shredded lettuce. Repeat prodecure for remaining ingredients. Serve immediately.

NOTE: Guacamole is also a good accompaniment for quesadillas.

Submitted by Territorial House Inc.

SUGGESTED USES FOR QUICK CUISINE

• Basil-Lime Vinaigrette: This makes an exceptional marinade for filet of fish, salmon, redfish, sole or boned and skinned chicken breast. Simply marinate for one hour and then grill or broil.
• Mushroom Sauce: Reduce by half and use as a poaching liquid for chicken, veal, pork or fish, then use as sauce for cooked meats. VARI-ATION: Add two tablespoons of sherry, port or a dry white wine before poaching. Reduce to desired consistency after meat is done and before putting sauce over meat.
• Sundried Tomato Pesto: Split and steam spaghetti squash until tender. Warm pesto in saute pan, add cooked squash and toss. VARIATION: Melt one tablespoon of Continental Herb Butter in saute pan, then add and warm pesto, add and toss squash.
• Green and Pink Peppercorn Mustard: Place two cups cream in a sauce pan and reduce by half. Add two to three tablespoons mustard and blend well. Use as a sauce for pork, beef, etc.
• Continental Herb Butter: Use as a sauteing medium in place of regular butter. Or soften and spread liberally over chicken, fish, pork or beef and then broil, roast or barbecue, basting with more as needed.

Submitted by TexaFrance

CRAWFISH ETOUFFEE

1½ sticks butter
4 lbs. crawfish tails
3 cans cream mushroom soup
3 cans celery soup
1 can cream onion soup

1 bunch celery, chopped
4 bell peppers, chopped
4 onions, chopped
Red pepper

Chop vegetables, saute in butter till tender. Add crawfish, cook out the water. Add soups. Simmer 15 to 20 minutes longer.

Submitted by Bernice Guillory, Crawfish Promotion Day Recipes
Texas A & M University System

NUTRIENT CONTENT OF CRAWFISH

For one (3½ oz.) serving:

Protein	19.4 grams
Fat	0.8 grams
Carbohydrates	0.0
Calories	85.0
Cholesterol	277.0 milligrams

Submitted by Texas A&M University

CRAWFISH PUFFS

3 lbs. crawfish tails
2 bell peppers
½ stalk celery
3 bunches green onions
2 bags croutons

12 slices garlic toast
4 jalapeno peppers
1 dozen eggs, beaten
Salt and black pepper, to taste

Run the first seven ingredients through a food chopper. Mix all together, drop by spoonfuls in hot oil.

Submitted by Dora Roy, Joe Heinen and Amos Roy, Crawfish Promotion Day
Texas A&M University System

CRAWFISH CREOLE A LA VIVYON

3 T. oil
3 T. flour
½ cup onion, chopped
½ cup celery, chopped
2 cloves garlic, chopped
1 can tomato sauce

1 can water
¼ cup green onions, chopped
⅛ cup parsley, finely chopped
1 lb. cleaned crawfish tails
Salt, black and red pepper to taste

Make a roux from oil and flour. Brown slowly. Add onion, celery and garlic. Saute in roux until transparent. Add tomato sauce and water. Simmer 45 minutes. Add green onions, parsley, crawfish tails, salt and peppers. If too thick, add a little more water. Simmer about 10 to 15 minutes. Serve over rice.

Submitted by Vivian Dorman, Crawfish Promotion Day, Texas A&M University

CRAWFISH CAULIFLOWER SALAD

1 lb. crawfish tails,	¼ cup chopped pimentos
2 cups cooked rice	1 tsp. salt
¾ head cauliflower, diced	Black pepper
½ cup green peppers, chopped	Sliced olives (green or black)
¼ cup chopped green onions	1 cup mayonnaise

Cook tails in crawfish boil seasonings or saute in butter with creole seasonings. Drain. Combine ingredients and toss lightly. Serve on cold lettuce leaf or scooped out tomatoes.

Submitted by Mae Dougharty, Crawfish Promotion Day Recipes, Texas A&M University

SPANISH RICE WITH CRAWFISH

1 box Spanish style Rice-Aroni	1 pkg. Taco seasoning
1 can (8 oz.) stewed tomatoes	1 lb. peeled crawfish tails
1 can (8 oz.) whole kernel corn, drained	

Follow directions on Rice-Aroni box, then before the rice simmers add tomatoes, corn, taco seasoning and crawfish. Let simmer on low for 25 minutes.

Submitted by Stephanie Kachtik, Crawfish Promotion Day, Texas A&M University

CRAWFISH BALLS

1 bunch green onions	2 eggs
1 big white onion, chopped	Cracker crumbs, as needed
4 stalks celery	Red pepper
1 large bell pepper	Salt and pepper
1 lb. crawfish tails	Garlic powder
4 cups cooked rice, cooled	Corn meal
1 stick butter, melted	Flour

Run vegetables through blender or food processor. Grind finely. Grind the crawfish tails real fine. Mix crawfish, onions and melted butter with eggs and add to cooked rice in a large bowl. Blend together by hand. If too moist, add cracker crumbs. Season with red pepper, salt and garlic powder. Make into balls (about the size of golf balls.) Mix cornmeal and flour together in equal parts. Roll crawfish balls in flour mixture and deep fat fry.

Submitted by Carol Daigle, Crawfish Promotion Day, Texas A&M University System

CRAWFISH ETOUFFEE A LA MUSHROOMS

2 lbs. cleaned crawfish tails and fat
2 sticks oleo
2 onions, chopped
1 bell pepper, chopped
3 or 4 stalks celery, chopped
3 or 4 pods garlic, crushed
¼ cup green onions, chopped (include tops)
¼ cup parsley, minced
2 cans cream of mushroom soup
Tony Chachere's Cajun Seasoning to taste
Red pepper (you want it "zingy")

Saute onions, bell pepper and celery in oleo until wilted. Add garlic, soup, onion tops and parsley and seasonings to taste. Add crawfish and cook about 10 minutes longer. Serve over rice.

Submitted by Mae Dougharty, Crawfish Promotion Day, Texas A&M University System

CRAWFISH AU GRATIN

2 bunches green onions
2 large regular onions
3 ribs celery
½ lb. butter
4 T. flour
1 large and 1 small can Pet milk
2 egg yolks, beaten well
11 oz. grated Cheddar cheese
2 lbs. crawfish

Chop vegetables fine. Saute onions and celery in butter. Add flour, blend well and then add both cans Pet milk and blend. Take off heat and add egg yolks and 8 oz. grated Cheddar cheese. Mix in crawfish. Blend well. Pour in casserole and top with 3 oz. grated Cheddar Cheese and bake at 350° until cheese is brown. (Approx. 20 minutes). NOTE: Crabmeat can be used in place of crawfish.

Submitted by Neola Menard, "Cooking with Crawfish"

CRAWFISH TAILS IN RUM

4 tsps. sugar
½ fifth rum
Juice of 1 lime
4 lbs. boiled crawfish
Seasonings

Clean tails and marinate in rum, lime juice and sugar for 30 minutes. Season to taste. Serve chilled or hot.

Submitted by Linda Harrison, "Cooking with Crawfish"

BOILED CRAWFISH

4 gal. water
4 onions, quartered
4 lemons, halved
1½ cup salt
½ cup vinegar
ground red pepper
15 lbs. live crawfish
Liquid or packaged crab boil

Purge crawfish, wash and discard dead ones. Combine water, onions, lemons and seasonings in a large pot. Bring to a boil. Add enough crawfish to raise liquid to within several inches of the top. Cover and

77

bring water back to a boil. Cook 3 to 6 minutes. (Crawfish should be bright red.) Strain crawfish, set aside. When liquid comes back to a boil, add more crawfish.

Submitted by "Cooking with Crawfish," Orange County Extension Agency

TEXAS DUET CHILI MIX

1 lb. lean cubed or ground beef, venison or pork
4 medium onions, chopped
1 can (8 oz.) tomato sauce
2 cans (16 oz. ea.) stewed tomatoes

4 to 7 T. chili mix (to taste)
2 tsp. apple cider vinegar
2 tsp. fresh cilantro, minced, optional
Salt to taste

Brown meat slightly. Add onion and simmer two minutes over medium heat. Add onions, tomato sauce, cilantro and vinegar. Simmer five minutes. Add remaining ingredients and cook over low heat, covered, for at least one hour. Add pinto beans (cooked) if desired. Package contents makes four to five recipes.

NOTE: This recipe was a first place winner at the 1986 International Food and Wine Show in San Francisco.

Submitted by Texas Duet

CORN TORTILLAS

1 cup stone ground corn meal (yellow, white, blue)
1 cup boiling water

2 to 2½ cups whole wheat flour
½ tsp. sea salt (optional)

Pour boiling water over the corn meal. Let sit for 10 minutes or more. Mix salt and whole wheat flour. Add enough flour to the corn meal mixture to make a kneadable dough. Knead for 5 to 10 minutes. Let rest for 5 minutes. Pinch off a piece of dough the size of a golf ball. Roll it out on a floured board to a more or less round shape about 4 inches in diameter. Cook on an unoiled hot griddle pan about two minutes per side or until lightly brown.

Submitted by Texas Fresh

TWO MELON SOUP

1 ripe cantaloupe, seeded and diced
2 T. fresh lemon juice
1 small honey dew melon, seeded and diced

2 T. fresh lime juice
1½ tsps. minced fresh mint or to taste

In a blender, puree the cantaloupe with lemon juice until mixture is smooth. Transfer the puree to a suitable container and refrigerate it, covered, for at least three hours. Rinse out blender and puree the honeydew with the lime juice and mint until mixture is smooth. Transfer the puree to a suitable container and refrigerate it, covered, for at least three hours. At serving time, transfer the purees to separate measuring cups or pitchers with pouring spouts. With one pitcher in each hand, simultaneously pour equal amounts of the puree into individual serving bowls. The purees will stay separated with the cantaloupe on one side and the honeydew on the other.

Submitted by Texas Fresh

TEXAS PECAN CRISPIES

1 cup butter
1 cup sugar
2 cups flour
1 tsp. vanilla

1 egg white
½ tsp. salt
1 cup chopped pecans

Cream together butter and sugar. Add flour and vanilla. Beat egg white to stiff peaks. Add salt. Fold egg whites into mixture. Add pecans. Drop by teaspoonfuls onto ungreased cookie sheet. Bake at 350° until lightly browned — about 20 to 25 minutes. Do not overcook.

Submitted by Texas Pecan & Gourmet Company

BEEF ENCHILADAS EMPALMADAS
(STACKED ENCHILADAS)

½ cup finely chopped onions
2 T. cooking oil
1 T. all purpose flour
½ cup milk
1 can (4 oz.) green chili peppers, rinsed, seeded and chopped
½ tsp. salt

2 cups diced cooked Texas Western Foods Marinated Beef Fajitas Strips (presliced)
2 tomatoes, peeled and chopped
2 T. cooking oil
3 corn tortillas (6 inch size)
1 cup (4 oz.) shredded Monterey Jack cheese

In skillet, cook onions in 2 T. oil till tender but not brown. Blend in flour. Add milk, chili peppers and salt. Cook, stirring constantly, till thickened and bubbly. Stir in beef and tomatoes. Heat through. Keep warm. In small skillet, heat 2 T. oil. Holding tortillas with tongs, dip in hot oil for 10 seconds or till limp. Drain on paper towel. Place a hot tortilla in a 9 by 9 by 2 inch baking pan. Top with about ¼ beef mixture and 2 T. cheese. Layer on remaining tortillas, beef mixture and cheese to make a stack. Bake in 350° oven for 20 minutes or till hot. Unstack to serve. Serves 4. EDITOR'S NOTE: Stack may also be cut in wedges for serving.

Submitted by Texas Western Foods Inc.

CHICKEN ENCHILADAS

1 pkg. (3 oz.) cream cheese,
   softened
1 T. milk
⅛ tsp. salt
¼ tsp. ground cumin (comino)
2 cups cooked, chopped Texas
   Western Foods Marinated
   Chicken Thigh, Breast or
   Tenderloins

6 flour tortillas (8 inch size)
1 can (10¼ oz) condensed cream
   of chicken soup
1 cup milk
8 pickled jalapeno peppers,
   rinsed, seeded and chopped
1 cup shredded Monterey Jack or
   Cheddar cheese (4 oz.)
1 carton (8 oz.) sour cream

In a bowl, combine softened cream cheese, 1 T. milk, salt and cumin. Add chopped, cooked chicken. Stir together until well combined. Spoon about ⅓ cup chicken mixture onto each tortilla near one edge. Roll up. Place filled tortillas, seam side down, in a greased 12 by 7½ by 2 inch baking dish. In a bowl, combine soup, sour cream, 1 cup milk, and the peppers. Pour mixture evenly over the tortillas in dish. Cover with foil. Bake in a 350° oven about 35 minutes or till heated thoroughly. Remove foil. Sprinkle enchiladas with cheese. Return to oven for 4 to 5 minutes or until cheese is melted. Makes 6 servings.

Submitted by Texas Western Foods Inc.

TOSTADAS DE POLLO
(Chicken Tostadas)

8 crisp tostadas shells (6 inch size)
2 pkg. (1 lb. each) Texas Western
   Foods Marinated Chicken
   Breast, Tenderloins or Thigh
¼ cup sliced green onions
2 T. butter or margarine
1 can (8 oz.) tomato sauce
½ tsp. garlic salt

½ tsp. salt
¼ tsp. ground cumin (comino)
2 cups shredded lettuce
1 cup shredded Monterey Jack
   cheese (4 oz.)
1 large avocado, seeded, peeled
   and sliced
½ cup sliced pitted ripe olives

Cut chicken meat into very thin strips. In medium skillet quickly cook chicken and onion in butter or margarine till chicken is done and onion is tender. Add tomato sauce, garlic salt, salt and cumin. Reduce heat and simmer, covered, for 15 to 20 minutes. To assemble: place a warm tortilla on serving plate, spoon on chicken mixture, then lettuce, cheese, avocado slices and olives. Drizzle with bottled hot sauce to taste if desired. Makes 8 servings.

Submitted by Texas Western Foods Inc.

TEX MEX MEAT PIE

2 T. oil
2 lbs. ground meat
1 onion, chopped
1 clove garlic, through press
5 T. Underwood's Texas Red Chili
   and Pinto Bean Seasoning
1 tsp. black pepper
1 can (15 oz.) ranch style beans
   (undrained)

14 slices American cheese or
   same amount of Velveeta
   cheese
1 can Campbell's Cream of
   Chicken Soup, mixed with 1
   can (10 oz.) Rotel Tomatoes,
   chopped
8 flour tortillas

Generously grease a 9 by 13 pan with shortening, (not "Pam"). Cook meat, onion, garlic with oil. Add Underwood's Texas Red and the black pepper. When meat is done, drain grease. Add beans, remove from heat and stir in gently. Set aside. Line bottom of greased pan with a layer of tortillas. Place a layer of cheese on top of tortillas, then put all of meat evenly on top of cheese. Add another layer of cheese on top of meat. Cover meat completely with tortillas and pour soup mixture over all. Bake at 350° for 30 minutes or until hot and bubbly. Slice in squares to serve. Serves 8.

Submitted by Underwood's Fine Foods

CHICKEN NACHOS

1 lb. chicken nuggets
1 cup cheese sauce
1 small can Rotel tomatoes

2 T. Underwood's Texas Red
Grated cheddar cheese

Fry or bake nuggets. In a saucepan, warm cheese sauce and add Rotel tomatoes and Texas Red. Dip nuggets in cheese sauce and layer in casserole. Top with grated cheese. Warm in oven until cheese melts. Serve warm.

Submitted by Underwood's Fine Foods

CHEESY CHILI CORNBREAD

1 recipe of your favorite
   cornbread batter
2 cups chili made with
   Underwood's Texas Red

½ cup grated cheddar cheese
1 small onion, chopped

In a 2 quart, greased casserole, pour in half of the cornbread batter. Spread chili on top, then sprinkle with cheese and the chopped onion. Top with remaining batter. Bake in 350° oven for 35 to 40 minutes or until cornbread is done.

Variation: Chopped jalapeno peppers may be added with the cheese and onion and chili.

Submitted by Underwood's Fine Foods

TEXAS RED CHILI

2 lbs. chili meat or ground beef   Water
½ cup Underwood's Texas Red
  Chili and Pinto Bean
  Seasoning

Barely cover meat with water. Add Texas Red seasoning and cook uncovered approximately 45 minutes to 1 hour.

Submitted by Underwood's Fine Foods

TEXAS RED CHILI MIXTURE
(For: chili pie, taco filling, taco salad,
enchiladas, and chili sloppy joes)

1 lb. ground beef	1 pkg. (3 oz.) cream cheese
1 green pepper, chopped	2 oz. cheese, grated
1 oz. Underwood's Texas Red	1 cup water
1 can (6 oz.) tomato paste	

Brown meat with pepper in skillet. Stir to crumble. Drain excess fat. Stir in Texas Red, tomato paste, cream cheese, cheese and water. Cook over medium heat, stirring, until mixture comes to a boil. Serve in any of the above dishes — or as a warm dip with corn chips.

Submitted by Underwood's Fine Foods

TEXAS RUB TUNA SALAD

1 can tuna, drained	lemon juice, to taste
¼ cup light mayonnaise	Underwood's Texas Rub (an all
2 carrots, grated	purpose dry seasoning), add
2 green onions, chopped	to taste

Sprinkle lemon juice on drained tuna. Add all other ingredients.

Submitted by Underwood's Fine Foods

TEXAS RUB MEATLOAF

1½ lbs. ground meat	1 small onion, finely chopped
1 egg	¼ cup celery finely chopped
¼ cup finely crushed buttery	1 T. catsup
crackers	2 tsps. Underwood's Texas Rub

Combine all ingredients and mix well. Spray loaf pan with vegetable coating and spread meatloaf evenly in dish. DO NOT COVER. Microwave at high heat 13 to 18 minutes, rotating dish ½ turn after half of cooking time. Test for doneness. Let stand uncovered for 5 minutes. Serves 4 to 6.

Submitted by Underwood's Fine Foods

TEXAS RUB OLD FASHIONED BEEF STEW

2 lbs. stew meat
¼ cup Underwood's Texas Rub
3 cups warm water

1 pkg. frozen stew vegetables
(fresh can be substituted)
1 can (16 oz) tomatoes

In saucepan, cover meat with water. Add Texas Rub and cook over medium heat for 45 minutes or until meat is tender. Add vegetables and cook until vegetables are tender. Add tomatoes and simmer 10 minutes. Serves 5 to 6.

Submitted by Underwood's Fine Foods

TEXAS RUB CRAB DIP

2 cups medium white sauce
8 oz. cream cheese
1½ T. lemon juice

2 tsps. Underwood's Texas Rub
1 lb. fresh or canned crab meat

Make medium white sauce. Add softened cream cheese and stir until smooth. Add lemon juice and Texas Rub and stir until well blended. Stir in crabmeat. Serve warm with chips, raw vegetables or crackers.

Submitted by Underwood's Fine Foods

TEXAS RUB ROAST CHICKEN OR TURKEY

1 large baking chicken or 1 turkey   Underwood's Texas Rub Dry
Seasoning and Marinate

Rinse chicken and pat dry. Sprinkle Texas Rub all over chicken, including inside cavity. Marinate in refrigerator from 2 to 6 hours. Place chicken in roasting pan and cover. Bake in preheated 350° oven for 1 hour. Remove cover. Baste and continue cooking one hour or until done.

Submitted by Underwood's Fine Foods

UNDERWOOD TEXAS RUB GRILLED MEATS

(Steaks — Hamburgers — Pork Chops — Chicken)

Sprinkle meats evenly on both sides with Texas Rub. Let marinate from 1 to 6 hours. Cook on barbecue grill or cook in oven or broiler, using natural juices to baste.

Submitted by Underwood's Fine Foods

FRENCH FRIED PEANUTS

Use only raw peanuts for this recipe.

Place peanut oil or vegetable oil in deep fryer. Heat fryer to 375°. Place in oil 12 oz. peanuts. Fry for 4 minutes. Remove and drain on paper towel. Salt to taste. Popcorn salt is recommended.

Submitted by Vanco Products Co.

PEANUT BRITTLE

2 cups white sugar
⅓ cup water
⅔ cups white corn syrup
2 cups RAW PEANUTS

2 T. butter
1½ tsp. soda
⅔ tsp. salt

Boil sugar, corn syrup and water until it spins a thread. Add peanuts and and stir continuously after peanuts are added. Cook until it turns a brownish gold. Remove from fire. Add butter, salt and soda. Pour onto buttered board to cool.

Submitted by Vanco Products Co.

COOK 'N FREEZE CHICKEN

8 to 10 lbs. deboned chicken
   breasts or drumsticks
1 jar (13 oz.) Van De Walle Fajita
   Marinade
4 to 6 cups water

1 jar (16 oz.) Van De Walle Very
   Mild, Medium or Extra Hot
   Picante Sauce
2 drops liquid smoke (optional)
Finely diced fresh onion
   (optional)

In a 4 quart sauce pan, mix the marinade, with 4 cups water and the picante sauce. Bring to a low boil, stirring constantly. Add liquid smoke and diced onions if desired. Add boneless chicken breasts to sauce and boil for at least 15 minutes, until meat is tender. Remove chicken and sear on a very hot grill or skillet until meat is browned. Serve remaining hot marinade sauce on side. Slice chicken into long strips and place in pan of simmering mixture for 5 minutes or until ready to serve.

TO SERVE: Remove from marinade sauce and wrap in warmed flour tortillas. Use remaining sauce for the fajitas. Top with Van De Walle Picante Sauce or Van De Walle Pico de Gallo.

TO FREEZE: Place cooked chicken in freezing bag or microwaveable container. Cover liberally with remaining marinade mix and seal container. Freeze.

TO SERVE FROZEN CHICKEN FAJITAS: Thaw to separate pieces. Simmer in marinade mix until meat is hot (stove or microwave.) Serve as above.

Submitted by Van de Walle Farms

LIVER EVEN YOUR KIDS WILL LIKE

1 to 1½ lbs. liver
¼ cup Van de Walle Fajita
   Marinade
¾ cup red wine
¼ cup cold water

1 bell pepper
1 onion, small, sliced
Salt and pepper to taste
Flour for dredging liver

For ease in handling, leave liver in large chunks. Slice into ½ inch thick slices. Sprinkle with salt and pepper and dredge in flour.

84

Mix Van De Walle Fajita Marinade wine and water in small bowl. Pour half of the mixture into large heated skillet. Add sliced liver, bell pepper and onion. Cook about 4 minutes on high heat. Pour remaining liquid into skillet and continue cooking on medium heat until liver loses its pink color and vegetables are tender crisp. Pan juices will form a thick rich gravy. Serve over rice. Serves 4 to 6.

Submitted by Van De Walle Farms

PAN FRIED VENISON

1½ lbs. venison steaks
¼ cup Van De Walle Fajita
    Marinade
¼ cup water

Salt and pepper (to taste)
Flour for dredging
Vegetable oil for frying

In shallow plastic or glass pan, mix marinade and water. Marinate venison in this mixture for 4 to 6 hours or overnight in refrigerator. In large skillet, heat enough oil to cover bottom of skillet. Remove venison from marinade and reserve liquid for use as gravy, if desired. Salt and pepper steaks lightly. Dredge in flour. Fry in hot oil 2 to 3 minutes each side, or until browned. Serves 4 to 6.

Submitted by Van De Walle Farms

STUFFED CABBAGE

12 large cabbage leaves, wilted
1 lb. ground meat (beef or pork
    or a mixture)
½ cup uncooked rice
3 T. Van De Walle Pico De Gallo
1 egg

¼ tsp. black pepper
1 can (8 oz.) tomato sauce
⅓ cup Van De Walle Mild Chip
    Dip
⅔ cup water

Pour boiling water over cabbage leaves to wilt. Mix meat, rice, pico de gallo, egg and black pepper. Place mound of meat mixture in wilted cabbage leaf. Fold over sides of leaf carefully and securely, pinning with toothpick. Mix remaining ingredients for sauce in separate bowl. In bottom of Dutch oven place 6 additional cabbage leaves to form base on which to place rolls. Place cabbage rolls seam side down. Pour sauce over rolls. Cover pan. Place sauce covered cabbage rolls in oven. Bake at 350° for about 1 hour. Remove lid and bake an additional 30 minutes. Add water, if needed. Serves 4 to 6.

Submitted by Van De Walle Farms

PARADISE HONEY PUMPKIN PIE

1 pkg. (8 oz.) cream cheese	1 tsp. cinnamon
¼ cup sugar	¼ tsp. ginger (or substitute 1½
½ tsp. vanilla	tsps. pumpkin pie spice for
1 egg	ginger and cinnamon)
1 unbaked (10 inch) pastry shell	Dash salt
¾ cup evaporated milk	2 eggs, slightly beaten
1¼ cups canned pumpkin	Honey
⅜ cup honey	Nuts

Combine softened cream cheese, sugar and vanilla. Mix until well blended. Add egg. Mix well. Spread onto bottom of pastry shell. Combine milk, pumpkin, honey, spices and eggs. Mix well. Carefully pour over cream cheese mixture. Bake at 350° for 1 hour and 15 minutes or until done. Cool. Brush with additional honey and garnish with nuts.

Submitted by Varsel Apiaries

VEGETARIAN CHILI

1 pkg. West brand chili mix	2 T. vegetable oil
1¼ cups combination dried pinto	⅞ cup boiling water
and kidney beans	Short grain brown rice, steamed
Water to cover beans	Cheese, shaved or grated
1 cup hamburger flavor textured	
vegetable protein (TVP)	

Place kidney and pinto beans (or beans of your choice) in pan and cover with water. Cook 1 to 1½ hours, being sure water is not completely absorbed, adding more as necessary. After beans are cooked, add boiling water to the TVP. Stir. Saute TVP mixture in vegetable oil. Add West brand chili mix. Then add beans with 2 cups water. Simmer 30 minutes, adding more water as needed. You may add chopped tomatoes or onions for different tastes. Serve on steamed short grain brown rice then top with cheese. Serves 6 to 8.

Submitted by West Brand Chili Inc.

"BIG D" FRITO PIE

1 pkg. West Brand chili mix,	1 8 oz. pkg. corn chips, crushed
cooked according to	1 small onion, finely chopped
directions with:	8 oz. Longhorn cheese, grated
2 lbs. ground meat	

Lightly grease a large casserole. Layer half the corn chips on the bottom. Add the onion in an even layer. Spread the chili over the onion. Sprinkle with remaining corn chips and top with grated cheese. Bake at 350° for 15 minutes or until cheese is melted and chili is bubbling. For variation, chopped tomatoes and shredded lettuce may be sprinkled over each serving. Serves 8 to 10.

Submitted by West Brand Chili Inc.

CHILI CON QUESO SALAD

1 pkg. West brand chili mix
2 lbs. ground meat
½ head of lettuce, chopped
2 tomatoes, chopped
1 onion, chopped or sliced
1 avocado, sliced

sliced green olives, as desired
1 lb. Velveeta cheese, with
½ can Ro-tel tomatoes with green
  chilies
Corn chips or tostados

Cook meat with chili mix according to directions. Mix next five ingredients together. Melt cheese and Ro-tel tomatoes in double boiler. Layer on a warm plate the following: corn chips or tostados, salad layer, chili, cheese mixture. Serve immediately. Serves 6 to 8.

Submitted by West Brand Chili Inc.

TEXAS CHILI DIP

1 pkg. West brand chili mix
2 lbs. ground meat
1 can (8 oz.) tomato sauce with
  bits

1 can Ro-tel tomatoes with green
  chiles
1 lb. Longhorn cheese, cut into
  small pieces

Cook meat with chili mix according to directions. Heat together with remaining ingredients in a double boiler, letting the cheese melt. Blend and serve very hot with corn chips or tostados. Serves 12.

Submitted by West Brand Chili Inc.

SAN ANTONIO SPECIAL

1 pkg. West brand chili mix 2 lbs.
  ground meat
1 lb. can stewed tomatoes

1 lb. can cream style corn
5 oz. raw egg noodles
American cheese, grated

Cook meat with chili mix according to directions. Mix with all other ingredients but the cheese and place in an oiled casserole. Then top with cheese. Bake for 20 minutes in 350° oven or until bubbly. Serves 8.

Submitted by West Brand Chili Inc.

CHUCK WAGON HOMINY PIE

1 pkg. West brand chili mix
2 lbs. ground meat
2 medium onions, sliced
1½ cups cracker crumbs

2 cans (1 lb. each) hominy,
  drained, reserving liquid
2 cups grated American cheese
Butter to dot

Cook meat with chili mix according to directions. Alternate layers of chili and hominy in a casserole, starting and ending with chili. Pour ½ cup hominy liquid over mixture. Arrange thin slices of onion, cover with grated cheese. Finish with cracker crumbs on top. Dot with butter and bake 20 to 25 minutes in 350° oven. Serves 8 to 12.

Submitted by West Brand Chili Inc.

SPICE PECANS

1 egg white, slightly beaten
2 T. water
½ cup sugar
½ tsp. salt

¼ tsp. cinnamon
¼ tsp. cloves
¼ tsp. allspice
2½ cups pecans

Add water to egg white. Mix remaining ingredients, except for pecans. Add to egg white mixture. Stir in pecans until well coated. Spread on greased cookie sheet and bake at 250° for 1 hour.

Submitted by Westside Orchard

SWEET N' CRUNCHY CORNBREAD

3 cups Arrowhead Mills high
  lysine cornmeal
1 cup Arrowhead Mills whole
  wheat pastry flour
Fresh sweet corn cut from 1 ear
  (approximately ⅔ cup)

¼ tsp. salt
2 T. Arrowhead Mills sesame oil
2 T. honey or barley malt (opt.)
2½ to 3 cups water
Sesame oil to oil baking dish

Preheat oven to 325°. Combine cornmeal, flour, sweet corn and salt. Add oil and sift in with hands. Add sweetener, if desired. Gradually add water until dough resembles a thick cookie batter. Oil a 9 by 13 inch baking dish. Heat the oiled dish in a 325° oven until hot but not smoking. Pour batter in pan and spread evenly. Bake for 30 minutes, then increase temperature to 350° for about 45 to 50 minutes or until light brown and top just begins to crack. Serve with Texas Pintos.

Submitted by Whole Foods Market

TEXAS PINTOS

1½ cups dry pinto beans
1 large onion, thinly sliced
2 large carrots in one inch chunks
3 ribs celery in ½ inch slices
1 bay leaf

1 tsp. cumin or Mexican
  seasoning
Water
Salt to taste

Soak beans in water 8 hours or use the quick soak method. Discard soaking water. Combine beans, vegetables, bay leaf, cumin and cover with water in a pressure cooker or soup pot. Pressure cook 45 minutes or bring to a boil and simmer 3 to 4 hours until done. (Watch the water level if not pressure cooking.) Season with salt and cook 10 more minutes. Serve with Sweet n' Crunchy Cornbread. Bring beans to a boil for 2 minutes. Remove from heat, and let sit, covered for 2 hours before cooking.

Submitted by Whole Foods Market

TEXAS WINE BRISKET

1 beef brisket

MARINADE:

1 T. garlic powder
1 T. black pepper
1 T. onion powder
½ cup vinegar

½ cup Worcestershire sauce
½ cup catsup
⅓ cup Wimberley Valley
  Notuveau Cabernet

Place brisket on foil (do not wrap). Cup foil around the edges. Pour marinade over brisket and refrigerate overnight. (Depending on size of brisket, you may need to double recipe.) Roll brisket up tight and bake at 350° for 4 to 5 hours. Slice and serve with a glass of Wimberley Valley Wine.

Submitted by Wimberley Valley Wines

TEXAS OVEN BARBECUED CHICKEN

1 broiler or fryer chicken, 2½ to
  3 lbs.
½ cup catsup
¼ cup WOODY'S Cook-in' Sauce

2 T. brown sugar
1 tsp. lemon juice
1 T. bourbon, optional

Cut chicken into pieces, thoroughly dry, place in plastic bag. Combine remaining ingredients, mixing well. Pour into bag and fasten securely. Refrigerate at least 4 hours or overnight, as desired, turning occasionally. Drain chicken, reserving marinade. Place on rack of broiler pan. Bake at 350° for 45 minutes or until tender, brushing with reserved marinade every 15 minutes. Makes 4 servings.

Submitted by Woody's Foods Inc.

ORIENTAL SKEWERED SHRIMP

¾ cup WOODY'S Sweet'n Sour
  sauce
4 tsps. soy sauce
⅛ tsp. ginger
1 lb. large shrimp, deveined
1 can (20 oz.) pineapple chunks,
  drained

1 bell pepper, (green, yellow or
  red) cut into 1 inch pieces
8 baby onions
1½ cups raw white rice, prepared
  according to package
  directions
8 skewers

Mix Sweet 'n Sour Sauce, soy sauce and ginger. Marinate shrimp in sauce 1 hour. Alternately slide shrimp, pineapple, pepper and onions onto 8 skewers. Baste with marinade. Grill or broil until shrimp is cooked as desired, about 3 minutes on each side. Baste with marinade when turning skewer. Serve over rice. Yield 4 servings.

Submitted by Woody's Foods Inc.

AUNT BETTY'S FAVORITE PORK CHOPS

1 medium onion cut into thin
   wedges
2 T. flour
1 can (8 oz.) tomato sauce
⅔ cup WOODY'S Sweet'n Sour
   Sauce

½ tsp. salt
6 boneless loin pork chops, cut ½
   inch thick, trimmed of
   visible fat
1 medium green pepper, cut into
   short, thin strips

Toss onion in flour. Add tomato sauce, Sweet'n Sour Sauce, and salt. Mix well. Place meat in single layer in shallow dish, pour sauce over meat. Cover and refrigerate at least 6 hours or overnight, as desired. Transfer meat and sauce to large skillet. Bring to a boil, reduce heat. Cover and simmer about 25 minutes or until meat is tender, adding green pepper during last 10 minutes of cooking. Remove meat from skillet; arrange on serving platter. Skim fat from skillet, cook and stir sauce about 1 minute to thicken, if necessary. Pour sauce over meat to serve. Makes 6 servings.

Submitted by Woody's Foods Inc.

CHUCKWAGON STEW

2 lbs. boneless beef stew meat, cut
   into 1 inch pieces
2 T. vegetable oil
1 can (13 or 14 oz.) beef broth
1¼ cups hot water
¾ cup WOOD'S Cook in' Sauce
1 medium onion, cut into ½ inch
   wedges
¼ cup chopped parsley
½ tsp. salt

1 can (16 oz.) stewed stomatoes
3 medium carrots, cut into 1 inch
   pieces
2 ears fresh or thawed frozen
   corn, cut into 1 inch pieces
   or 1 pkg. (10 oz.) frozen corn
2 medium red potatoes, cubed,
   (peeled if desired)
¼ cup cold water
2 T. flour

In a 3 quart pot with lid brown meat, half at a time, in hot oil. Return all meat to pot. Add broth, hot water, ½ cup of Cook in' Sauce, onion, parsley, and salt. Bring to a boil, reduce heat. Cover and simmer 1 hour or until meat is tender. Add tomatoes and juice to stew with carrots, corn and potatoes. Cover and simmer 25 minutes or until vegetables are tender. In separate bowl, gradually add cold water to flour, mixing until smooth. Stir in remaining Cook 'in Sauce. Gradually stir into stew. Heat to boiling, stirring constantly. Boil and stir 1 minute or until thickened. Makes 6 to 8 servings, about 10 cups stew.

Submitted by Woody's Foods Inc.

WOODY'S BAKED BRISKET

5 lbs. well trimmed boneless beef
   brisket

1 jar (13 oz.) WOODY'S Cook in'
   Sauce

Trim fat from meat leaving ⅛ inch layer on top. Score and pierce on both sides at 1 inch intervals. Place meat in 9 by 13 inch baking pan. Spread ½ jar sauce on each side. Turn fat side up. Cover tightly. Marinate a minimum of 5 hours or overnight. Bake covered at 250° for 5 hours or until tender. Cut meat at slanted angle across the grain into thin slices. Serve with pan drippings. Makes 8 to 10 servings. NOTE: Add 30 minutes cooking time for each additional pound when using larger brisket.

Submitted by Woody's Foods Inc.

COWBOY BOB'S MEAL IN A POT

½ lb. ham, cut into bite size peices
2 cans (15 oz. each) pinto beans,
   undrained
2 medium onions, coarsely
   chopped
1 medium green pepper, cut into

¾ inch pieces
1 cup tomato juice
½ cup WOODY'S Cook in' Sauce
1 tsp. chili powder
¼ cup chopped fresh cilantro,
   optional

Combine all ingredients except cilantro in a large saucepan. Bring to a boil. Cover and simmer 20 minutes. Top with cilantro. Makes 6 to 8 servings, about 8 cups stew.

Submitted by Woody's Foods Inc.

GLAZED CHICKEN WINGS

12 chicken wings
⅓ cup catsup

⅓ cup WOODY'S Sweet'n Sour
   Sauce
½ tsp. soy sauce

Cut wings at joints; discard wing tips. Dry thoroughly with paper towels. Combine catsup, Sweet'n Sour Sauce and soy sauce. Mix well. Pour into plastic bag, and add chicken. Place in refrigerator at least 1 hour or up to 24 hours, turning bag occasionally. Drain chicken, reserving marinade. Place on rack of broiler pan. Brush chicken with reserved marinade; turn and brush again with marinade. Bake at 350°. Continue baking, brushing with marinade every 10 minutes or until tender, about 30 minutes. Serve additional sauce as a dipping sauce. Make 24 appetizers.

Submitted by Woody's Foods Inc.

SOUTHWEST STYLE BEANS

4 slices bacon
½ cup chopped onion
⅓ cup WOODY'S Cook in' Sauce
¼ cup catsup

2 T. brown sugar
2 cans (16 oz. each) pork and
   beans in tomato sauce

Cook bacon in medium skillet until crisp. Drain. Reserve 2 T. drippings. Cook onion in reserved drippings until tender but not brown. Crumble bacon, add to skillet with Cook in' Sauce, catsup and brown sugar. Mix well. Add beans. Bring to a boil. Reduce heat and simmer uncovered about 15 minutes or until thickened to desired constistency. Makes 6 to 8 servings, about 4 cups beans.

Submitted by Woody's Foods Inc.

91

BARBECUED SHORT RIBS

6 lbs. meaty beef short ribs,
trimmed of visible fat
1 cup WOODY'S Cook in' Sauce
1 cup catsup

1 T. lemon juice
1 medium onion, finely chopped
1 T. vegetable oil

Combine Cook in' Sauce, catsup, and lemon juice. Saute onion in oil. Stir into sauce. Brush over ribs. Marinate at least 5 hours or overnight. Arrange ribs on rack in large baking pan. Cover tightly and bake at 250° for 5 hours or until tender, basting hourly. Makes 4 to 6 servings. NOTE: Ribs vary in size and meat content so cooking time may vary.

Submitted by Woody's Foods Inc.

SMOKY CHEESE SPREAD

2 cups (8 oz.) shredded sharp
cheddar or Swiss cheese
¼ cup mayonnaise

¼ cup WOODY'S Cook in' Sauce
3½ T. milk

Combine ingredients in blender container. Blend until smooth, stopping blender to scrape down sides as necessary. Chill. Serve as a spread for crackers or dip for vegetables. Makes about 1½ cups.

Submitted by Woody's Foods Inc.

HILL COUNTRY BAKED FISH

1 lb. orange roughy fish fillets, or
other mild whitefish
1 egg, slightly beaten
¼ cup WOODY'S Cook-in' Sauce,
divided

1 cup finely crushed tortilla or
corn chips
2 T. green onion slices
1 can (16 oz.) tomatoes

Dry fish thoroughly. Preheat oven to 450°. Combine egg and 2 tablespoons sauce. Dip fish into egg mixture, coat with chips. Place on well greased baking sheet. Bake 8 to 10 minutes or until fish flakes easily when tested with fork. While fish bakes, drain tomatoes, reserving juice. Coarsely chop tomatoes, then combine with juice and remaining sauce in small saucepan. Simmer 5 minutes, stirring occasionally. To serve, spoon sauce over baked fish, then sprinkle with green onions. Serves 4.

Submitted by Woody's Foods Inc.

CHICKEN ON A STICK

2 large whole chicken breasts,
   boned, skinned and split
⅔ cup La Martinique True
   French Vinaigrette

⅔ cup WOODY'S Sweet 'n Sour
   Sauce

Pound chicken between 2 sheets of plastic wrap to ½ inch thickness. Cut each into 1 inch wide strips. Place in plastic bag. Combine French Vinaigrette and Sweet 'n Sour Sauce, mixing well. Pour into bag with chicken. Press out air and fasten securely. Refrigerate 1 hour, turning bag frequently. Drain chicken, reserving marinade. Thread chicken on to skewers, accordion style. Place over hot coals or on rack of broiler pan. Brush generously with marinade. Grill or broil about 6 to 8 minutes or until chicken is cooked through, turning and basting frequently with marinade. Bring remaining marinade to a boil in small saucepan. Serve with chicken. Makes 4 servings. NOTE: Bottled Italian dressing may be substituted for vinaigrette.

Submitted by Woody's Foods Inc.

HONEY PECAN PIE

1 cup honey
4 eggs
¼ tsp. salt
1 tsp. vanilla

1 T. butter
1 cup pecans
1 unbaked (9 inch) pie shell

Pour honey into an iron skillet and bring to a boil. Beat eggs well and slowly add hot honey, stirring constantly. Add salt, vanilla and pecans. Pour into pie shell, cut butter into small pieces and dot top of pie. Bake at 400° for 10 minutes. Reduce heat to 300° and bake 20 minutes longer.

Submitted by Youngblood's Honey Inc.

OSGOOD PIE

4 eggs, separated
2 cups sugar
3 tsp. vinegar
1 tsp. cloves
1 tsp. cinnamon

2 T. melted butter
½ cup raisins
½ cup chopped dates
1 cup chopped pecans
⅛ tsp. salt

Beat the egg yolks and combine with other ingredients except egg whites. Beat egg whites until stiff and fold lightly into mixture with wire whip or slotted spoon. Pour into 2 unbaked 8 or 9 inch pastry shells. Bake at 300° or 325° for 35 minutes.

Submitted by Mrs. G.G. Conoley of Taylor

LEMON PECAN CAKE

3 cups sugar
3 sticks butter or oleo
3 cups flour
9 eggs

1 lb. candied pineapple
1 lb. candied cherries
1 qt. pecans
2 oz. lemon extract

Soak pecans overnight in lemon extract. Cream sugar and butter. Add eggs one at a time. Beat in flour. Add remaining ingredients. Bake in 325° oven until lightly browned and springy (about 45 minutes). Makes 2 cakes.

Submitted by Martha Hill Vermillion, Athens, Tex.

CRAB PETS

1 can (16 oz.) blackeyed peas,
 undrained
3 cups rich chicken broth

1 large onion, chopped
Cornbread
1 raw egg

Puree peas. Cook in broth with onion to a rolling boil. Add enough cornbread to make a consistency of dressing. Mix in egg. Place in crab shells and bake till lightly browned on top. This recipe was a prize winner at the Annual Blackeyed Pea Jamboree in Athens, Tex.

Submitted by Martha Hill Vermillion, Athens, Tex.

MENUS

TEXAS INDEPENDENCE DAY

Chili (see Index)
Texas Pintos (page 88)
Cornbread (page 88) and Saltine Crackers
Relish tray with pickles, relishes, chopped onions, tomatoes and
    peppers
Shredded cheese
Old Fashioned Buttermilk Pie (page 73)
Beer

FOURTH OF JULY

Grilled Steaks or Barbecue
Potato Salad and Cole Slaw (See Index)
Tortillas or Bread
Fresh Watermelon or Homemade Ice Cream
(Peach, Pecan or Blueberry, see Index)
Bloody Marias (page 55) or Texas Red Sangria (page 41)

NEW YEAR'S DAY

Blackeyed Peas (See Index)
Matagorda Oysters on the half shell
Assorted Appetizers (See Index)
Muffins and Cornbreads (See Index)
Green Chile Stew (page 73)
Berry Steeped Chocolate Cake (page 23) or Lemon Pecan Cake
      (pages 3, 94)
Bloody Marias (page 55) or Texas Champagne

JUNETEENTH

Fried Chicken or Fish, use regular batter or Mexican style (page 69)
      or Shiner beer batter (page 69)
Hotwater cornbread or Spicy Hushpuppies (page 68)
      or Sweet 'N Crunchy cornbread (page 88)
Turnip greens or Mustard Greens
or
Blackeyed Peas cooked fresh and made into Texas Caviar (page 52)
Sliced tomatoes
Corn on the cob or Corn relish (page 52)
Sweet Potato Pie (or use Sweet Potato Souffle, page 6)
Beer or Iced Tea (see page 42)

EASTER MENU

Ham glazed with Sweet Pepper Relish or Texas Wine Jelly
  or Jalapeno Jelly or any Texas Jelly, Jams or Preserves
Asparagus — or Green Beans (See page 5, 11, or 63)
Stuffed Eggs, (page 48 or 61)
Macaroni n' Cheese (page 62)
or
Nutty noodles (page 57)
or
Macaroni Salad (page 11)
or
Fideo pronto (page 60)
Fresh Mixed Green Salad (page 26)
or
Sassy Spinach Salad (page 39)
Honey Bran Muffins (page 13) or Sorghum Bran Muffins (page 16)
  or Six Weeks Bran Muffins (page 38) or
Pepper Relish Surprise Corn Muffins (page 8)
Strawberry shortcake or other Berry or Fruit dessert (See Index)
Texas Citrus punch (page 11)

THANKSGIVING MENU

Roast Turkey with Cornbread Stuffing (see page 47)
Peach halves stuffed with Red Pepper Relish (see page 8)
Cranberry Salad Mold (see page 39)
Sweet potatoes in orange halves or Sweet potato souffle, (page 5)
Potatoes and gravy
Rolls
Paradise Honey pumpkin pie (page 86) or mince pie
  or Almond Pumpkin Charlotte (page 43)
Texas Wine or Champagne

CHRISTMAS

Turkey with Lantana Oyster stuffing (page 47) and giblet gravy
or
Tex-Mex Roast Turkey (or Chicken) stuffed with tamales (page 83)
Festive Frozen Cranberry Salad (page 39)
Asparagus casserole (page 5) or Asparagus with Rarebit Sauce
    (page 63)
or
Pecan Broccoli (page 56)
Crusty Sweet Potato Casserole (page 5)
Relish Tray
Dinner Rolls or Corn Tortillas (page 78)
Osgood Pie (page 94) or Fruit Cake (page 28)
    or Holiday Eggnog Pie (page 40)
Texas Spritzer (page 67) and/or Winter Warmers (page 45)

Editor's Note: Texans vary in their traditional menus for Christmas. For most, the menu is more or less the same as for Thanksgiving, except that they may add an extra meat such as ham or roast beef to accompany the turkey. Others (particularly in the German community) favor a duck for Christmas. The Mexican-Americans, however, traditionally have tamales during the Christmas season. Therefore, I have included an alternative with the Mexican flavor.

CINCO DE MAYO

Barbecued Lamb or Goat (page 72)
Seven Layer Salad (page 8)
Squash and Cheese casserole (page 62)
Flour or Corn tortillas (page 78)
Buttered Pecan Ice Cream (page 38)
Texas Wine or Texas Beer

DIES Y SEIS DE SEPTIEMBRE

Two Melon Soup (page 78)
Fajita Ranch Style Party Dip (page 71)
Fajitas (pages 25, 55, 71, 85) and Quesadillas (page 74)
Tortillas (page 78)
Guacamole (page 53)
Salsa Picante (page 53)
Sour Cream, Grated Cheese, Chopped Onions, Jalapenos,
    and Tomatoes
Fruit Compote with Poached Pears (page 71)
Beer or Iced Tea

Index of Recipes

106

Poached with fruit compote, 71

Peas, see Blackeyed and Beans

Pecan

Broccoli, pecan, 56
Baked fish
Buttered pecan ice cream, 38
Lemon pecan cake, 3, 94
Nutty noodles, 57
Orange pecandy, 57
Pecan brittle, 37
Pie,
   Ina's, 27
   Honey, 42
   Pape's, 56
   Ribboncane, 15
Salad, pecan vegetable, 57
Spinach casserole, 56

Pheasant

Roasted with apple sauce and ham
   compote 35

PIES

Dessert

Blueberry cheesecake, 32
Blueberry coconut, 37
Blueberry cream cheese, 33
Blueberry, fresh, 13
Buttermilk, old fashioned, 73
Eggnog cream, holiday, 40
Lemon sour cream pie, 39
Osgood pie, 93
Pecan pie, 15, 27, 42, 56
Honey pumpkin, 86

Main Dish

Chili, 12
Golly tamale, 51
Hominy pie, pork, 87
Sausage supper, 20

Pork

Chops, Aunt Betty's favorite, 90

Fajitas, 55
"Paisano" barbecue, 50
Ribs, peach glazed, 32
Stew "fricasse," 31

Potato, see Sweet potatos and
   Salads

Pumpkin

Almond Pumpkin Charlotte, 43
Paradise honey pumpkin pie, 86

SALADS

Cheese salads, 53, 54
Chicken, satay, 46
Clam cottage cheese, 40
Crab and avocado, 27
Cranberry, 39
Duck, 34
Guacamole, 55
Julienne, chef's, 26
Macaroni and ham, 27
Macaroni, Theresa's, 11
Marinated, 21
Mixed green, 26
Mozzarella and Tomato, 53
Mushroom rice, 47
Okra, 73
Pecan vegetable, 57
Potato:
   Bavarian, 43
   Chef's, 27
   Theresa's, 10
Sausage, 20
Seven layer, 8
Slaw, 8
Spinach, 46
Springtime, 39
Texas cheese salads, 54
Vegetable, pecan, 57

Sauce and salsa

Butter, herbed, 46
Chile con queso, 52
Fajita marinade, 71

PRODUCT CATEGORIES

Seasonings/Chili Mixes
Adams Extract Co.
Adkins Seasoning Co.
Ben's Speciality Food & Spices
Bolner's Fiesta Products, Inc.
Caliente Chili, Inc.
Dallas International Marketing
Desert Smoke Products, Inc.
El Paso Chile Co., The
Hoyt's Texas Chili
J. P.'s Enterprises
Janet's Own Home Sweet Home
La India Packing Company
Lantana Seasoning
Limon Bakery
Mr. Bar-B-Q, Inc.
Nellie Corporation
Paso-Pak Chili Company, Inc.
Ramage Farms
Red Eye Company
San Antonio River Mill
South Texas Spice Co., Inc.
Texas Western Beef
Twelve Oaks
Underwood's Fine Foods
Van De Walle Farms, Inc.
West Brand, Inc.
Winn's Good Cooking

Sauces / Relishes / Dips
Amigos Canning Co., Inc.
Angel Craft, Inc.
Bobby Free Farms, Inc.
Brazos Beef Emporium, Inc.
Caliente Chili, Inc.
Claude's Sauces, Inc.
Country Classic Foods
Cox's Relish Co., Inc.
Dickie Davis Sweet & Hot
Goldin Pickle Co., Inc.
Hast Foods Co.
Hell On The Red, Inc.
Hill Country Foods, Inc.
Janet's Own Home Sweet Home
Knapp-Sherrill Co.
L-C Food Products Co.
Laredo Red, Inc.
Lazy Susan, Inc.

Mr. Bar-B-Q, Inc.
Nellie Corporation
New Canaan Farms
Pace Foods, Inc.
Pedro Gatos Salsa, Inc.
Pet, Inc., Old El Paso Foods
Rico Products
Senor Pepe, Inc.
Soupcon Corportion
Tejas Specialties
TexaFrance/Custom Catering
Texas Duet
Texas Prairie, Inc.
Van De Walle Farms, Inc.

Nuts / Seeds / Peanuts
Aldus Co.
Bluebonnet Apiaries, Inc.
Brazos Valley Orchards
Cokendolpher Orchard
Comanche Golden
Crawford Pecans, R. H.
Dee & C Pecans
El Paso Chile Co., The
Frog House, The
Madden Pecan Co.
Nuts To You Inc.
Pape Pecan House
Peach Basket
Pecan Producers, Inc.
Pecan Shed
Pecan Valley Nut Company, Inc.
Picosos Peanut Co., Inc.
Poor Farm, The
Quality Peanut Warehouses, Inc.
Ramage Farms
Rico Products
San Saba Pecan, Inc.
Serendipity Of The Valley
Spear Orchard
Sunbelt America
Texas Pecan & Gourmet Co.
Traylor Farms, Inc.
Tucker's Farm & Craft
Valentine Co., Inc.
Vanco Products Co., Inc.

Weidenfeller Trading Co.
Westside Orchard
Young's Home Orchard
Zeys Of Texas

Dairy Products / Cheeses / Shortenings
Alpine Frozen Specialties, Inc.
Amy's Ice Creams
Anderson Clayton Foods
El Paso Cheese Co.
Gandy's Dairies, Inc.
Garza Baking Co.
Houston Dairy
Hygeia Dairy Company
Land O' Pines
M-G, Inc. Egg Division
Maxim Egg Farms, Inc.
Mozzarella Company
Pace Foods, Inc.
Purity Ice Cream Mfgr.
Superior Dairies
Swiss Pride Dairies
Vandervoort Dairy Foods Co.

Meats / Meat Products
B3R Country Meats, Inc.
Bar-B Foods
Big Texan Steak Ranch
Bismillah Tx Halal Meat Co., Inc.
Brazos Beef Emporium, Inc.
Cap Ranch Meat Market & Smokehouse
Carlton Food Products, Inc.
Cedar Mountain Buffalo Company
Dimmitt Meat Co.
Double L Ranch, The
Eddy Packing Co., Inc.
Edes Custom Meats
Fischer's Meat Market
Fred's Steak House
Fredericksburg Lockers, Inc.
Frontier Meat & Supply
Geronimo Sausage Co.
Gonzalez Packing Co.
Gooch Packing Co.
H & H Foods
Handy Packing Co.
Hans Mueller Sausage
Hickory House Bar B-Que
Hubbell & Sons Food Products, Inc.
Huntsville Meats, Inc.
J-B Foods
Lad-Pak, Inc.
LaGrange Meat Market, Inc.

Laxson Provision Co.
Meat Link: Rancher to Retail
Monterey House, Inc.
Newman Meats, Inc.
Palo Duro Meat, Inc.
Pedro's Tamales
Plantation Foods, Inc.
Producer Perfect Beef
R & B Quail Farm
Ranch House Meat Co.
Rayner Packing Co.
Riker Farm
S & D Holmes Smokehouse, Inc.
Sadler's Bar-B-Que Sales, Inc.
Sam Kane Beef Processors, Inc.
San Antonio Packing Co.
Serloin Shops Of Stephenville, Inc.
Sklar's Frozen Food Center, Inc.
Smokey Denmark Sausage Co.
Sunday House Foods, Inc.
Sunrise Ranch
Sysco Food Services
Tekita House Foods, Inc.
Texas Western Beef
Texas Wild Game Cooperative
Texham, Inc.
Thompson Farms, Inc.
Triple C Meats
Twelve Oaks
Union Slaughter, Inc.
Uvalde Meat Processing
Valley Wholesale Meat Co. Inc.
Valley Wholesale Meat Co. Inc. II
Wolf Brand Products
Woody's Meats, Inc.
Yoakum Packing Co.
Zero Food Locker

Flour / Corn Meal / Mixes / Sugar
Burrus Milling, Dept. of Cargill
Flatland Mills
Imperial Sugar Co.
Lamb's Grist Mill
Morrison Milling Co.
Pioneer Flour Mills

Tortillas / Taco Shells / Chips
Bellville Potato Chip Factory
Bernard's Tortilla Factory
Cavazos' Sons, Inc.
El Azteca Tortilleria
El Galindo, Inc.
El Rio Tortillas
El Tepeyac
Garza Baking Co.
Jasso's Tortillas And Bakery

La Malinche Tortilla / Tamale
  Factory
Mayan Tortillas
Mexico Bakery, Inc.
Monterey House, Inc.
Old Mexico Bakery, Inc.
Pet, Inc., Old El Paso Foods
Rico Products
Ruiz Tamale & Tortilla Factory
Ruthie's Chip Corporation
Tejano Products

Baked Goods
Blossom Bakery, Inc.
Brazos Blue Ribbon Products
Collin Street Bakery
Custom Fortune Cookie Co.
Dutch Regale Bakery, Inc.
Eilenberger's Butter Nut Baking
  Co.
Gladys' Cookie shop
Glen-Mary Farms
Gourmet Unique
Jasso's Tortillas And Bakery
Kilkenny Cakes
La Parisienne French Bakery, Inc.
Limon Bakery
Lone Star Bakery, Inc.
Miss King's Kitchen
Neal's Cookies
New York, Texas Cheesecake
Old Peanut Butter Warehouse
Sonja's Internat'l. Confections
Texas American Cookie Co.
Texas Duet
Texas Ya-Hoo Cake Co.
Zita's

Fresh Produce
Ambrosia Orchards
Anderson Produce
Barrett Produce Co.
Barrett-Fisher Co.
Barron's Blueberries
Bill's Veges
Blueberry Lane Farm
Blue Diamond Farm
Blueberry Patch
Brazos Valley Orchards
Buckaroo Blueberry Ranch
C & A Sales, Inc.
Calco of Houston, Inc.
Catlett Creek Berry Farm
Chaparral Fruit Sales, Inc.
Cokendolpher Orchard
Colville & Wilson, Inc.

Constanzo Bordano Farms
Corn Growers, Inc.
Dad's Crawdad Farm & Berry
  Patch
Das Peach Haus
De Bruyn Produce Co.
Diamond Farm
E & B Peach Orchard
Eastex Farms
El Kay Farms
Energy Sprouts, Inc.
Fincastle Nursery & Farms
Four J's Orchard
Fredericksburg Orchards, Inc.
Fresh Farm Produce, Inc.
Frio Foods, Inc.
G. D. Produce
Green Grove Citrus
H & S Produce Company
Haak Vineyards
Hamilton Blueberry Farm
Harvey, Robert E.
Helle Tomato Co. Inc.
Hoelscher Farms
Home Grown Sprout Co., The
Huff, W. L.
Johnson Farms
King Tom Tomato Farms
Lazy D Berry Farm, Inc.
Lee's Blueberry Haven
Lily's
Longhorn Mesquite
Lyles Produce Farm
Maxwell Orchards
Meek Ag Products
Morrison, Glen
Mott Blueberry Hill Farms
O. L. Rozell Peach Farms
Olton Produce, Inc.
Pape Pecan House
Patty's Herbs, Inc.
Peach Basket
Pedernales Valley Orchard &
  Farms
Plainview Produce, Inc.
Plantation Pines Berry Farm
Poor Farm, The
Progressive Groves, Inc.
Ramage Farms
Reinauer & Sons, Inc., E. C.
Rhew Peach Orchard
Richards Horticulture
Riddick Farms
Russell Vineyards

111

Sand Pit Enterprises, Inc.
Sandy Foot Farm
Sandy Hill Farm
Sem-Tex Produce
Sky Line Growers
Smith's Peach Farm
Southern Blues Farm
Spear Orchard
Spring River Farm
Sterling Orchards
Sunset Vineyard & Nursery
Supreme Products, Inc.
Tangram Nursery
Texas Best Produce
Texas Blueberry Marketing Group
Texas Blueberry Plantation
Texas Fresh
Tucker's Farm & Craft
Twelve Oaks
Valley Farmers Co-op
Van De Walle Farms, Inc.
Weidenfeller Trading Co.
Westside Orchard
Woodrum Produce
Young's Greenhouses
Young's Home Orchard
Zeys Of Texas

Canned Goods
Allen Canning Co.
Amigos Canning Co., Inc.
Knapp-Sherrill Co.
L-C Food Products Co.
Lucky Peas, Inc.
Millie's Kountry Kitchen
Pet, Inc., Old El Paso Foods
Rex & Johnnie's Little Acre
Talk O' Texas Brands, Inc.
Taormina Co.

Beverages
Ambrosia Orchards
Artesia Waters, Inc.
Bluebonnet Hill Winery, Inc.
Chateau Montgolfier Vineyards
Cypress Valley
Dr. Pepper Bottling Co. North TX
Fall Creek Vineyards
G. Heileman Brewing Co., Inc.
Guadalupe Valley Winery
Hill Country Cooler, Inc.
Hill Country Spring Water Of Tx
Knapp-'Sherrill Co.
La Escarbada XIT Vineyard &
   Winery
Llano Estacado Winery, Inc.

Mariano's Specialty Products
Messina Hof Wine Cellars
Oberhellmann Vineyards
Pheasant Ridge Winery
Piney Woods Country Wines
Preston Trail Winery
Richland Beverage Corp.
Richter Wine Group, Inc.
Sanchez Creek Vineyards
Skweezins Corporation
Southwest Citrus, Inc.
Specialty Processing Corp.
Spoetzl Brewery, Inc.
Ste. Genevieve Vineyards
Sundor Corp.
Tejas Vineyard & Winery
Texas Citrus Exchange
Texas Vineyards Inc.
Val Verde Winery
Wimberley Valley Wines, Inc.

Honey / Syrup
B & Mc Enterprises
Baker Apiaries
Billman's Honey Farm
Blackland Apiaries Honey
Bluebonnet Apiaries, Inc.
Bost Apiary, Robert & Mary
Brockett-Tyree Farms
Buckaroo Blueberry Ranch
Buddy's Pure Natural Honey
Burke's Busy Bee Farm
Catlett Creek Berry Farm
D & P Honey
Dad's Crawdad Farm & Berry
   Patch
Good Flow Honey & Juice Co.
Green Apiaries, Russell
H. C. Honey House
Happy Honey Co.
Hoyt's Honey Farm
J & R Texas Honey
Jeff House Family
Johnny Boy's Honey
Lenz Apiary
Lone Star Honey Co.
Mary's Miel
Oliver's Honey
Orr's Apiaries, Bobby
Ramage Farms
San Antonio River Mill
Sandwoods Farm
Serendipity Of The Valley
Southern Gold Honey Co.

112

Texas Bee Company-Varsel
Apiaries
Texas Duet
Texas Fresh
Texas Honey Co-Op Inc.
Texas Natural Gifts Honey Co.
Tule Creek Apiary
Weaver & Sons
Weaver Apiaries, Inc.
Youngblood Honey, Inc.

Jams and Jellies
Angel Craft, Inc.
Catlett Creek Berry Farm
Das Peach Haus
Lazy Susan, Inc.
Little Red Hen Pantry, Inc.
New Canaan Farms
Reba's Country Cupboard
Roaring Springs Jam Factory
San Antonio River Mill
Serendipity Of The Valley
Soupcon Corporation
Tejas Specialties
TexaFrance / Custom Catering
Texas Duet
Texas Jellies
Texas Original Mesquite Jelly
Texas Ya-Hoo Cake Co.

Candy
Atwood Candy Company
Crawford Pecans, R. H.
Fredericksburg Fudge
Jesse's Honey Crunch
La King's Confectionery
Monterey House, Inc.
Old Peanut Butter Warehouse
Pipecreek Texas Bullcorn
Segovia Mexican Candy
Snacks and Candies, Inc.
Texas Bess
Truly Delicious Candies
Tyler Candy Co., Inc.
Webb's Candy Co.

Mesquite Wood
Desert Smoke Products, Inc.
Flippen Industries
Flying W Wood
Halley's Mesquite Chunks
Indian Creek Mesquite, Inc.
J. P. Mesquite Co.
Lone Star Mesquite
Longhorn Mesquite
Menard Mfg. & Distb. Co.
Mickle, Inc.

P & W Mesquite Co., Inc.
Primarily Barbecue
Quality Texas Products, Inc.
Smokemaster Products, Inc.
South Texas Mesquite Corp.

Rice
Dad's Crawdad Farm & Berry
Patch
Doguet Rice Milling Co.
Farms Of Texas
Jeff House Family
Lindsey Rice Mill, Inc.
Pedro's Tamales
Texas Crawfish Farmers
Association
Texas Fruit Baskets
Van De Walle Farms, Inc.
Wolf Brand Products

Miscellaneous
Amy's Food Co.
Baker Apiaries
Bellville Potato Chip Factory
Calco of Houston, Inc.
Carter Processing
Chef A. Joseph Products, Inc.
Comet American Marketing
Common Market, The
Corn Growers, Inc.
El Campo Rice Milling Co.
Farms Of Texas
Fenton Egg Farm
Fisherman's Harvest, Inc.
G. A. T. Inc.
H & S Seafood
Haak Vineyards
Herbal Gems
Kenneth Henneke Humpback
Bluecat
La Escarbada XIT Vineyard &
Winery
Little Red Hen Pantry, Inc.
Lone Star Honey Co.
Midway Fish Farm
Monterey House, Inc.
Mott Blueberry Hill Farms
Nature's Herbs
O. B. Macaroni Co.
Old Peanut Butter Warehouse
Perry Products
Pheasant Ridge Winery
Plantation Pines Berry Farm
Textray
Val Verde Winery
Weaver & Sons

TASTE OF TEXAS COMPANIES

Adams Extract Co.
P.O. Box 17008, Austin, TX 78760
(512) 282-1126 Jim McDonald

Adkins Seasoning Co.
P.O. Box 764213, Dallas, TX 75376
(214) 339-5096 Paul Adkins

Aldus Co.
1619 S. Kentucky D-1000
Amarillo, TX 79102
(806) 353-9953 Tom Martin

Allen Canning Co.
P.O. Box 250, Siloam Spring, AR 72761
(501) 524-6431 David Allen

Alpine Frozen Specialities, Inc.
1317 N. Medicine, Dallas, TX 75203
(214) 942-1680 Daniel L. Brackeen

Ambrosia Orchards
Route 1, Box 227
Arthur City, TX 75411
(214) 732-4568 Robert Parsons

Amigos Canning Co., Inc.
224 Wilmot, San Antonio, TX 78237
(512) 434-0433 Beverly J. Velasco

Amy's Food Co.
3818 Reveille St., Houston, TX 77087
(713) 645-7305 Phyllis Hsu

Amy's Ice Creams
3403 Guadalupe, Austin, TX 78705
(512) 458-6895 Robert Wilder

Anderson Clayton Foods
P.O. Box 660037, Dallas, TX 75266
(214) 450-6128 John Brewster

Anderson Produce
Box 391, Gorman, TX 76454
(817) 734-2886 Deroy Anderson

Angel Craft, Inc.
Rt. 3, Box 424, Taylor, TX 76574
(512) 352-3257 Joy Angel

Artesia Waters, Inc.
4671 Walzem Road
San Antonio, TX 78218
(512) 654-0293 Rick M. Scoville

Atwood Candy Company
1408 Avenue O, Plano, TX 75074
(214) 423-3688 Thomas W. Atwood

B&Mc Enterprises
P.O. Box 19007, Fort Worth, TX 76119
(817) 429-1046 Frank A. McAnulty

B3R Country Meats, Inc.
Box 374, Childress, TX 79201
(817) 937-9870 Minnie Lou Bradley

Baker Apiaries
Rt. 4, Box 240-B, Elgin, TX 78621
(512) 856-2704 Gary R. Baker

Bar-B Foods
Route 1, Box 5300, Lufkin, TX 75901
(409) 824-2213 Steven R. McClure

Barrett Produce Co.
Box 447, Muleshoe, TX 79347
(806) 272-4546 Lynne Box

Barrett-Fisher Co.
P.O. Box 750, Hereford, TX 79045
(806) 364-1680 Wesley S. Fisher

Barron's Blueberries
Rt. 6, Box 370, Lindale, TX 75771
(214) 882-6711 Mike Barron

Bellville Potato Chip Factory
412 E. Main St., Bellville, TX 77418
(409) 865-9374 Wendell M. Ward

Ben's Speciality Food & Spices
P.O. Box 8428, Fort Worth, TX 76124
(817) 457-1240 Ben Richardson

Bernard's Tortilla Factory
P.O. Box 2955, Midland, TX 79702
(915) 682-9136 Albert Valles

Big Texan Steak Ranch
P.O. Box 37000, Amarillo, TX 79101
(806) 372-7000 R. J. Lee, Jr.

Bill's Veges
4312 Erie, Midland, TX 79703
(915) 694-3676 Billie Schneider

Billman's Honey Farm
Rt. 1, Box 211 BLM
San Antonio, TX 78223
(512) 635-7084 Ervin L. Billman

Bismillah Tx Halal Meat Co., Inc.
6411 Elmwood Ave
Lubbock, TX 79424
(806) 794-1800 Gulbano Suleman

Blackland Apiaries Honey
P.O. Box 395, Prosper, TX 75078
(214) 347-2371 David Whetsel

Blossom Bakery, Inc.
42 Lamar Park Shopping Center
Corpus Christi, TX 78411
(512) 857-2736 Bruno Courtin

Bluberry Lane Farm
Rt. 1, Box 1161, Spruger, TX 77660
(409) 963-1878 James Frazee

Blue Diamond Farm
P.O. Box 703, Alamo, TX 78516
(512) 787-7887 Rene Garza

Blueberry Patch
SR 2, Box 751, Silsbee, TX 77656
(409) 385-1200 Lamar Lynch

Bluebonnet Apiaries, Inc.
P.O. Box 1840, McAllen, TX 78501
(512) 968-5709 Henry Graham

Bluebonnet Hill Winery, Inc.
P.O. Box 243, Ballinger, TX 76821
(915) 365-2781 Antoine Albert

Bobby Free Farms, Inc.
Route 3, Box 100, Muleshoe, TX 79347
(806) 965-2131 Bobby Free

Bolner's Fiesta Products, Inc.
426 Menchaca St.
San Antonio, TX 78207
(512) 734-6404 Michael J. Bolner

Bost Apiary, Robert & Mary
Route 3, Box 60
Georgetown, TX 78626
(512) 863-3656 Robert H. Bost

Brazos Beef Emporium, Inc.
700 South Bryan St., Bryan, TX 77803
(409) 776-0298 Craig D. Conlee

Brazos Blue Ribbon Products
1301 BFM 2818
College Station, TX 77840
(409) 693-2137 Bob Hedderman

Brazos Valley Orchards
919-A N. Valley Mills Dr.
Waco, TX 76710
(817) 662-6562 Brad Harris

Brockett-Tyree Farms
9410 Gatetrail Dr., Dallas, TX 75238
(214) 348-3024 Jerry L. Brockett

Buckaroo Blueberry Ranch
P.O. Box 489, Scottsville, TX 75688
(214) 935-3736 James G. Newman

Buddy's Pure Natural Honey
2803 Seagoville Rd.
Seagoville, TX 75159
(214) 287-2345 James E. Parker

Burke's Busy Bee Farm
608 Silas St., Sweetwater, TX 79556
(915) 235-3660 Jimmie Burke

Burrus Milling, Dept. of Cargill
P.O. Box 79370, Saginaw, TX 76179
(817) 232-1160 David Darling

C & A Sales, Inc.
6115 Denton Drive-Suite 127
Dallas, TX 75235
(214) 351-6125 Phillip M. Garcia

Calco of Houston, Inc.
2400 Dallas St., Houston, TX 77003
(713) 236-8668 Kent Wang

Caliente Chili, Inc.
P.O. Drawer 5340, Austin, TX 78763
(512) 472-6996 Tom Nall

Cap Ranch Meat Market & Smokehouse
Route 5, Box 5080, Mineola, TX 75773
(214) 569-2822 David Simms

Carlton Food Products, Inc.
P.O. Box 311385
New Braunfels, TX 78131
(512) 625-7583 Bill Campbell

Carter Processing
2nd and Ave R, Sunray, TX 79086
(806) 948-4441 J. Morris Carter

Catlett Creek Berry Farm
Rt. 4, Box 1062, Decatur, TX 76234
(817) 627-3308 M. Gayle Moore

Cavazos' Sons, Inc.
601 North Pino St., Weslaco, TX 78596
(512) 968-2585 Jesus C. Cavazos

Cedar Mountain Buffalo Company
P.O. Box 12940, Odessa, TX 79768
(915) 563-9554 Larry G. Lee

Chaparral Fruit Sales, Inc.
P.O. Box 21366
San Antonio, TX 78221
(512) 626-3600 Mario Lopez

Chateau Montgolfier Vineyards
P.O. Box 12423, Fort Worth, TX 76116
(817) 448-8479 Henry C. McDonald

Chef A. Joseph Products, Inc.
7878 Querida Lane, Dallas, TX 75248
(214) 991-5977 Aurel Joseph

Claude's Sauces, Inc.
900 B-1 Hawkins, El Paso, TX 79915
(915) 778-7343 Glenda Castaneda

Cokendolpher Orchard
Rt. 4, Box 284, Wichita Falls, TX 76301
(817) 544-2242 O. W. Cokendolpher

Collin Street Bakery
401 W. 7th Street, Corsicana, TX 75110
(214) 872-8111 John Crawford

Colville & Wilson, Inc.
P.O. Drawer 193, Hereford, TX 79045
(806) 364-3131 Dwight C. Colville

116

Comanche Golden
P.O. Box 392, Comanche, TX 76442
(915) 356-3161 John E. Williams

Comet American Marketing
P.O. Box 1681, Houston, TX 77001
(713) 447-5053 Karen Tigert

Common Market, The
1610 San Antonio, Austin, TX 78701
(512) 472-1900 Mark Yznaga

Constanzo Bordano Farms
Rt. 1, Box 114-A, Atascosa, TX 78002
(512) 622-9639 Debbie Constanzo

Corn Growers, Inc.
Batesville Route. #1147
Uvalde, TX 78801
(512) 278-1309 Bert McCasland

Country Classic Foods
254 Lollock Dr., Devine, TX 78016
(512) 663-2908 Carroll Ley

Cox's Relish Co., Inc.
P.O. Box 680, Daingerfield, TX 75638
(214) 645-2701 Connie Cox Naron

Crawford Pecans, R. H.
Rt. 1, Box 146, Arthur City, TX 75411
(214) 732-4440 David H. Ferguson

Custom Fortune Cookie Co.
2523 Fairway Pk. Dr., #518
Houston, TX 77092
(713) 683-6139 Bonnie Chow Gutierrez

Cypress Valley
P.O. Box 128
Round Mountain, TX 78663
(512) 825-3333 Dale G. Bettis

D & P Honey
2607 Woodline
San Antonio, TX 78251
(512) 684-8843 Dave Tuttle

Dad's Crawdad Farm & Berry Patch
P.O. Box 248, Martindale, TX 78655
(512) 357-6623 Albert H. Cobb, Sr.

Dallas International Marketing
915 Nance Drive, Irving, TX 75060
(214) 254-5693 Charlene Sauer

Das Peach Haus
Route 3, Box 118
Fredericksburg, TX 78624
(512) 997-7194 Case D. Fischer

De Bruyn Produce Co.
Box 2171, Hereford, TX 79045
(806) 364-3263 Lee W. Drake

Dee & C Pecans
Rt. D, Box 537, Lamesa, TX 79331
(806) 489-7645 Cathy Broyles

Desert Smoke Products, Inc.
7007 Twin Hills, Suite 400
Dallas, TX 75231
(806) 259-3554 Edwin G. Jones

Diamond Farm
Rt. 4, Box 206-A
Grand Saline, TX 75140
(214) 962-4779 Duane Goff

Dickie Davis Sweet & Hot
Box 937, Menard, TX 76859
(915) 396-4421 Clara Treadwell

Dimmitt Meat Co.
200 N. Broadway, Dimmitt, TX 79027
(806) 647-3210 V. C. Hopson

Doguet Rice Milling Co.
795 S. Major Drive
Beaumont, TX 77707
(409) 866-2297 Mike Doguet

Double L Ranch, The
Rt 1, Box 362, Waelder, TX 78959
(512) 839-4545 R. M. Lockhart

Dr. Pepper Bottling Co. North TX
P.O. Box 655024, Dallas, TX 75265
(214) 579-1024 John K. Custer

Dutch Regale Bakery, Inc.
3922-B Woodbury Dr.
Austin, TX 78704
(512) 442-7879 Irene Kranenburg

E & B Peach Orchard
Rt. 2, Box 128-B, Hempstead, TX 77445
(409) 826-6303 Brenda McKnight

Eastex Farms
Rt. 5, Box 377, Rusk, TX 75785
(214) 683-5726 B. Bradshaw

Eddy Packing Co., Inc.
Box 392, Yoakum, TX 77995
(512) 293-2361 Larry Rutledge

Edes Custom Meats
Rt. 5, Box 305, Amarillo, TX 79118
(806) 622-0205 Melvin Edes

Eilenberger's Butter Nut Baking Co.
512 N. John St., Palestine, TX 75801
(214) 729-2176 Tom Broyles

El Azteca Tortilleria
611 San Enrique, Laredo, TX 78040
(512) 723-7093 Raul Quijano

El Campo Rice Milling Co.
101 S. Washington St.
El Campo, TX 77437
(409) 648-2696 R. L. Van Amburgh

El Galindo, Inc.
1216 E. 6th St., Austin, TX 78702
(512) 478-5756 Thomas Galindo, Jr.

El Kay Farms
60 Kinkaid East
Montgomery, TX 77356
(713) 623-0515 Larry K. Burton

El Paso Cheese Co.
7002 Commerce Ave.
El Paso, TX 79915
(915) 778-9486 Fred Villalba

El Paso Chile Co., The
100 Ruhlin Court, El Paso, TX 79922
(915) 544-3434 N. Kerr

El Rio Tortillas
910 E. 6th Street, Austin, TX 78702
(512) 476-0945 Manuel Barberena

El Tepeyac
1602 Santa Maria Ave.
Laredo, TX 78040
(512) 722-9330 Gilbert Lopez

Energy Sprouts, Inc.
3602 Highpoint
San Antonio, TX 78217
(512) 654-3963 Jane Phipps

Fall Creek Vineyards
1111 Guadalupe St., Austin, TX 78701
(512) 476-4477 Ed Auler

Farms Of Texas
P.O. Box 1305, Alvin, TX 77512
(713) 331-6481 Deborah Locke

Fenton Egg Farm
Rt. 5, Post 20 Box 7
Lake Brownwood, TX 76801
(915) 752-7191 Fred Barnett

Fincastle Nursery & Farms
Rt. 2, Box 169, Larue, TX 75770
(214) 675-4022 Donald Cawthon

Fischer's Meat Market
304 N. Main, Muenster, TX 76252
(817) 759-4211 John C. Fischer

Fisherman's Harvest, Inc.
Route 2, Box 754, Anahuac, TX 77514
(409) 355-2296 Doris Nelson

Flatland Mills
HCR 1, Box 26, Dimmitt, TX 79027
(806) 647-4289 Bryce Dowell

Flippen Industries
9400 N. Cen. Expwy., #1606
Dallas, TX 75231
(214) 361-1535 David Ellis

Flying W Wood
P.O. Box 117
Richland Springs, TX 76871
(915) 452-3295 Jimmy Decker

Four J's Orchard
Rt. 1, Box 652, Wichita Falls, TX 76301
(817) 855-4366 Johnny L. Roberts

Fred's Steak House
1201 E. Marshall, Longview, TX 75601
(214) 236-3122 Lee C. Cummings

Fredericksburg Fudge
126 Industrial Loop
Fredericksburg, TX 78624
(512) 997-2133 John Honigschmidt

Fredericksburg Lockers, Inc.
P.O. Box 487
Fredericksburg, TX 78624
(512) 997-3358 Wayne Edwards

Fredericksburg Orchards, Inc.
1607 Hwy 290 E.
Fredericksburg, TX 78624
(512) 997-9820 Mert Togen

Fresh Farm Produce, Inc.
1133 Austin Highway
San Antonio, TX 78209
(512) 822-4450 Ken Herzig

Frio Foods, Inc.
P.O. Box 367, Uvalde, TX 78801
(512) 278-4525 Joe Gerber, Jr.

Frog House, The
Rt. 4, Box 275 FM 171
Wichita Falls, TX 76301
(817) 544-2427 Beverlee Kurtz

Frontier Meat & Supply
1462 Austin Highway
San Antonio, TX 78209
(512) 824-7467 Jimmie W. Huizar

G. A. T. Inc.
P.O. Box 249, La Villa, TX 78562
(512) 262-1355 Manuel B. Gonzalez

G. D. Produce
633 Fairway Rd., Waco, TX 76710
(817) 772-7349 Gregory De Leon

G. Heileman Brewing Co., Inc.
100 Harborview Plaza
La Crosse, WI 54601
(608) 785-1000 Tom Macauley

Gandy's Dairies, Inc.
332 Pulliam St., San Angelo, TX 76903
(915) 655-6965 Garland Holloway

Garza Baking Co.
6130 Ridgebrook St.
San Antonio, TX 78250
(512) 434-0523 David C. Garza

Geronimo Sausage Co.
2119 Price Court, Laredo, TX 78040
(512) 723-1468 Jeromino Villareal

Gladys' Cookie Shop
Route 1, Box 281-A
Flatonia, TX 78941
(512) 865-3682 Gladys Farek

Glen-Mary Farms
Rt. 4, Box 935, Jefferson, TX 75657
(214) 562-1011 M. G. Watts, Jr.

Goldin Pickle Co., Inc.
9219 Diplomacy Row
Dallas, TX 75247
(214) 638-0271 Stephen Collette

Gonzalez Packing Co.
3090 San Antonio Hwy.
Eagle Pass, TX 78852
(512) 773-5337 Vidal Gonzalez

Gooch Packing Co.
P.O. Box 2738, Abilene, TX 79604
(915) 673-8222 Larry Nichols

Good Flow Honey & Juice Co.
2601 E. 1st Street, Austin, TX 78702
(512) 472-6714 Tom Crofut

Gourmet Unique
2030 Ave. G, #1108, Plano, TX 75074
(214) 422-0609 Rick Hulkenberg

Green Apiaries, Russell
P.O. Box 164, Ector, TX 75439
(214) 961-4247 Russell L. Green

Green Grove Citrus
2115 W. Highway 83
McAllen, TX 78501
(512) 686-9566 Hector J. Villarreal

Guadalupe Valley Winery
1720 Hunter Road
New Braunfels, TX 78130
(512) 629-2351 Donna L. Lehr

H & H Foods
P.O. Box 389, Mercedes, TX 78570
(512) 565-6366 Ruben E. Hinojosa

H & S Produce Company
P.O. Box 401, Hart, TX 79043
(806) 938-2121 Sue Hawkins

H & S Seafood
Box 1585, Aransas Pass, TX 78336
(512) 758-1820 Terry Holden

H. C. Honey House
104 Arrowhead Lane
Schertz, TX 78154
(512) 658-4800 Herbert Cloud

Haak Vineyards
6318 Ave. T, Santa Fe, TX 77510
(409) 925-3496 Raymond L. Haak

Halley's Mesquite Chunks
1007 White Sands, Katy, TX 77450
(713) 392-0282 Robert Chappell

Hamilton Blueberry Farm
2115 Wilson Lake
Livingston, TX 77351
(409) 563-4910 John W. Hamilton

Handy Packing Co.
P.O. Box 2420, San Angelo, TX 76902
(915) 653-2308 Jerry Stokes

Hans Mueller Sausage
2459 Southwell, Dallas, TX 75229
(214) 241-2793 Steve Cash

Happy Honey Co.
2080 Edson Drive
Beaumont, TX 77706
(409) 892-4481 Robert Nolan

Harvey, Robert E.
Rt. 1, Box 120, Nixon, TX 78140
(512) 582-1063 Robert E. Harvey, Jr.

Hast Foods Co.
10827 Caprock, Dallas, TX 75218
(214) 343-0459 Wayne Hast

Hell On The Red, Inc.
Route 1, Box 8-K
Telephone, TX 75488
(214) 664-2573 T. R. Baugh

Helle Tomato Co Inc
P.O. Box 1137, Mission, TX 78572
(512) 585-4521 G. T. Helle, Jr.

Herbal Gems
Box 775, Frankston, TX 75763
(214) 876-2130 Gem Rigsby

Hickory House Bar B-Que
630 W. Woodard, Denison, TX 75020
(214) 463-3600 John Doyle

Hill Country Cooler, Inc.
5858 Westheimer, Suite 404
Houston, TX 77057
(713) 789-8720 Thomas Wolfe

Hill Country Foods, Inc.
2520 Electronic Ln. #803
Dallas, TX 75220
(214) 350-3370 Francis E. Hunter

Hill Country Spring Water Of TX
10715 Gulfdale, #140
San Antonio, TX 78216
(512) 525-8151 Hank Forrest

Hoelscher Farms
HC 34, Box 184, Midland, TX 79701
(915) 535-2300 Jerome H. Hoelscher

Home Grown Sprout Co., The
P.O. Box 377, Tulia, TX 79088
(806) 995-2320 Jerry Herndon

Houston Dairy
P.O. Box 2503, Houston, TX 77252
(713) 523-3661 Conrad W. Zwerneman

Hoyt's Honey Farm
11711 I-10 East, Bayton, TX 77520
(713) 576-5020 Hoyt Page

119

Hoyt's Texas Chili
P.O. Box 4399, Dallas, TX 75208
(214) 948-3093 Wm. H. Patterson, Sr.

Hubbell & Sons Food Products, Inc.
415 E. Hamilton, Houston, TX 77076
(713) 695-6855 Bart Henderson

Huff, W. L.
Rt. 1, Box 175, Call, TX 75933
(409) 423-3665 W. L. Huff

Huntsville Meats, Inc.
P.O. Box 636, Huntsville, TX 77340
(409) 295-5415 Dick Wharton

Hygeia Dairy Company
P.O. Box 751, Harlingen, TX 78551
(512) 423-2050 Donald R. Smith

Imperial Sugar Co.
P.O. Box 9, Sugar Land, TX 77487
(713) 491-9181 Robert Guffey

Indian Creek Mesquite, Inc.
Rt. 3, Box 162-A
Brownwood, TX 76801
(915) 643-2650 Freddy E. Carter

J & R Texas Honey
4508 Biscayne Dr.
Fort Worth, TX 76117
(817) 281-1552 John M. Myers

J-B Foods
Box 7, Waelder, TX 78959
(512) 665-7511 Ronald Beeman

J. P. Mesquite Co.
1014 South Oak, Pearsall, TX 78061
(512) 334-8361 Pete T. Espinsoa

J. P.'s Enterprises
P.O. Box 1676, Brazoria, TX 77422
(409) 964-3572 Judy G. Peters

Janet's Own Home Sweet Home
1101 Dalton Lane, Austin, TX 78742
(512) 385-4708 Janet Morgan

Jasso's Tortillas And Bakery
502 N. Closner, Edinburg, TX 78539
(512) 383-3319 Cresencio Jasso

Jeff House Family
103 Forest Brook Dr.
Red Oak, TX 75154
(214) 849-2529 Cynthia House

Jesse's Honey Crunch
P.O. Box 63146, Pipe Creek, TX 78063
(512) 535-4736 Sherry Curtis

Johnny Boy's Honey
6710 Highway 66, Rowlett, TX 75088
(214) 475-3314 Donald Monroe

Johnson Farms
Route One, Knox City, TX 79529
(817) 658-3144 Donald Johnson

Kenneth Henneke Humpback Bluecat
Rt. 1, Box 54, Hallettsville, TX 77964
(512) 798-5934 Kenneth Henneke

Kilkenny Cakes
3703 Kerbey Lane, Austin, TX 78731
(512) 499-0209 Gayle M. Browne

King Tom Tomato Farms
3400 FM 1518
Guadalupe County, TX 78154
(512) 658-4522 Donald Holmberg

Knapp-Sherrill Co.
P.O. Drawer E, Donna, TX 78537
(512) 464-2442 David McDaniel

L-C Food Products Co.
P.O. Box 610612, Austin, TX 78761
(512) 343-2159 G. W. Chandler

La Escarbada XIT Vineyard & Winery
P.O. Box 1070, Hereford, TX 79045
(806) 364-7020 Arthur R. Reinauer

La India Packing Company
1520 Marcella Avenue
Laredo, TX 78040
(512) 723-3772 Hilda R. Acre

La King's Confectionery
2323 The Strand, Galveston, TX 77550
(409) 762-6100 Jack H. King

La Malinche Tortilla/Tamale Factory
702 South Port
Corpus Christi, TX 78405
(512) 884-7883 Rosario Carrizo

La Parisienne French Bakery, Inc.
900 Vargas, Austin, TX 78741
(512) 385-1310 Alice Limon

Lad-Pak, Inc.
P.O. Box 368, Needville, TX 77461
(409) 793-6210 Jody Duyka

LaGrange Meat Market, Inc.
P.O. Box 520, LaGrange, TX 78945
(409) 249-5858 Robert J. Gacke

Lamb's Grist Mill
Rt. 1, Box 66, Hillsboro, TX 76645
(817) 582-2405 Louise Lamb

Land O' Pines
500 Abney, Lufkin, TX 75901
(409) 634-3227 Joel A. Grambrell

Lantana Seasoning
P.O. Box 1837, New Caney, TX 77357
(713) 689-6441 Glen Soulliere

Laredo Red, Inc.
P.O. Box 12930, Fort Worth, TX 76116
(817) 870-1425 Robert E. Brown

Laxson Provision Co.
P.O. Box 9043, San Antonio, TX 78204
(512) 226-8397 Robert E. Laxson

Lazy D Berry Farm, Inc.
Rt. 1, Box 443, Winnie, TX 77665
(409) 296-2882 Barbara Devellier

Lazy Susan, Inc.
1702 S. Presa, San Antonio, TX 78210
(512) 534-1330 John Reeves

Lee's Blueberry Haven
Rt. 1, Box 417-B, Silsbee, TX 77656
(409) 385-5179 Clarence Lee

Lenz Apiary
4702 Debbie, San Antonio, TX 78222
(512) 648-2579 Will F. Lenz

Lily's
Rt. 5, Box 299-A, Canton, TX 75103
(214) 567-2832 Bobby Joe Lander

Limon Bakery
900 Vargas Road, Austin, TX 78741
(512) 385-1310 Alice Limon

Lindsey Rice Mill, Inc.
P.O. Box 118, Waller, TX 77484
(409) 372-2807 C. M. Lindsey

Little Red Hen Pantry, Inc.
Box 543, Port Neches, TX 77651
(409) 727-4570 Elizabeth Mead

Llano Estacado Winery, Inc.
P.O. Box 3487, Lubbock, TX 79452
(806) 745-2258 John Lowey

Lone Star Bakery, Inc.
3430 E. Commerce
San Antonio, TX 78220
(512) 223-3434 William T. Scott

Lone Star Honey Co.
17 Fair Oaks, Leander, TX 78641
(512) 259-0524 Don Atkins

Lone Star Mesquite
1201 China, Abilene, TX 79602
(915) 672-5145 Ray Wadle

Longhorn Mesquite
P.O. Box 244, Luling, TX 78648
(512) 875-2265 C. R. Kohutik

Lucky Peas, Inc.
P.O. Box 2160, Athens, TX 75751
(214) 677-1188 Donald W. Moeller

Lyles Produce Farm
Route 2, Box 302, Alba, TX 75410
(214) 765-2481 Preston Lyles

M-G, Inc. Egg Division
P.O. Box 697, Weimar, TX 78962
(409) 725-8576 George W. Kloesel

Madden Pecan Co.
6104 Cholla Dr., Fort Worth, TX 76112
(817) 451-3535 Bette Robinson

Mariano's Specialty Products
1200 Executive Dr. E., #129
Richardson, TX 75081
(214) 644-5287 Tom TenBrink

Mary's Miel
2800 Oak Crest, Austin, TX 78704
(512) 441-0190 Mary Cullinane

Maxim Egg Farms, Inc.
Rt. 1, Box 31, Boling, TX 77420
(713) 342-6651 Vincent Reina

Maxwell Orchards
HCR 5, Box 30, Dimmitt, TX 79027
(806) 647-4613 Dale Maxwell

Mayan Tortillas
2720 Zacatecas, Laredo, TX 78043
(512) 723-6269 Raul Quijano

Meat Link: Rancher to Retail
Rt. 1, Box 419, Waelder, TX 78959
(512) 540-4881 Shirley E. Frazier

Meek Ag Products
207 N.E. Alpine, Plainview, TX 79072
(806) 293-9459 Marvin Meek

Menard Mfg. & Distb. Co.
Box 654, Menard, TX 76859
(915) 396-2141 Lee Stafford

Messina Hof Wine Cellars
Route 7, Box 905, Bryan, TX 77802
(409) 778-9463 Paul or
Merril Bonarrigo

Mexico Bakery, Inc.
P.O. Box 1595, Kingsville, TX 78363
(512) 592-8536 J. O. Alvarado

Mickle, Inc.
10008 Gilson Lane, Houston, TX 77086
(713) 444-4841 W. R. Mickle

Midway Fish Farm
Rt. 2, Iowa Park, TX 76367
(817) 855-3711 Jeff Watts

Millie's Kountry Kitchen
Route 3, Box 484, La Grange, TX 78945
(409) 247-4256 Millie Petras

Miss King's Kitchen
5302 Hwy. 75 N., Sherman, TX 75090
(214) 893-8151 Ivan Papier

Monterey House, Inc.
3310 South Richey
Houston, TX 77017
(713) 943-2626 Dana Spaeth

Morrison Milling Co.
Box 719, Denton, TX 76202
(817) 387-6111 Paul E. Ishee

Morrison, Glen
Box 827, Stanton, TX 79782
(915) 756-3682 Glen Morrison

Mott Blueberry Hill Farms
P.O. Box 293, Spurger, TX 77660
(409) 429-3196 Margie E. Mott

Mozzarella Company
2944 Elm Street, Dallas, TX 75226
(214) 741-4072 Paula S. Lambert

Mr. Bar-B-Q, Inc.
P.O. Box 750, Rosebud, TX 76570
(817) 583-7597 Billie Wiesser

Nature's Herbs
2415 Glen Ivy, San Antonio, TX 78213
(512) 341-1118 Mary Dunford

Neal's Cookies
423 Southwest Freeway
Houston, TX 77002
(713) 520-6602 Neal Elinoff

Nellie Corporation
P.O. Box 1088, Royse City, TX 75089
(214) 635-9222 C. M. Stephenson

New Canaan Farms
P.O. Box 386
Dripping Springs, TX 78620
(512) 858-7669 Tim W. Tingle

New York, Texas Cheesecake
Rt. 2, Box 220
LaRue/New York, TX 75770
(214) 675-3485 Evelyn C. Dunsavage

Newman Meats, Inc.
Box L, Brenham, TX 77833
(409) 836-3152 R. A. Newman

Nuts To You Inc.
309 N. Beltline #115, Irving, TX 75061
(214) 790-3101 Bill Brewer

O. B. Macaroni Co.
P.O. Box 53, Fort Worth, TX 76101
(817) 335-4629 Louis J. Laneri

O. L. Rozell Peach Farms
Rt. 22, Box 378, Tyler, TX 75704
(214) 592-2074 Orvice L. Rozell

Oberhellmann Vineyards
Llano Rt. Box 22
Fredericksburg, TX 78624
(512) 685-3297 Robert P. Oberhellman

Old Mexico Bakery, Inc.
3900 Woodbury Dr., Austin, TX 78704
(512) 441-9198 Elizabeth G. Rivera

Old Peanut Butter Warehouse
100 20th Street, Galveston, TX 77550
(409) 762-8358 Susan L. Stubbs

Oliver's Honey
105 West Billington, Waco, TX 76706
(817) 662-6583 Charles E. Oliver

Olton Produce, Inc.
P.O. Box 751, Olton, TX 79064
(806) 285-2472 Billie R. Waldrip

Orr's Apiaries, Bobby
1312 Woodway, Hurst, TX 76053
(817) 284-3904 Bobby Orr

P & W Mesquite Co., Inc.
Box 235, Knox City, TX 79529
(817) 658-3587 Don Thompson

Pace Foods, Inc.
P.O. Box 12636
San Antonio, TX 78212
(512) 224-2211 R. J. Sands

Palo Duro Meat, Inc.
P.O. Box 31117, Amarillo, TX 79120
(806) 372-5781 Richard Rexroat

Pape Pecan House
P.O. Box 1281, Seguin, TX 78155
(512) 379-7442 Kenneth Pape

Paso-Pak Chili Company, Inc.
P.O. Box 969, Fabens, TX 79838
(915) 764-3716 Jay Petersen, Jr.

Patty's Herbs, Inc.
Rt. 1, Box 31J, Pearsall, Tx 78061
(512) 334-3944 Patricia M. Johnson

Peach Basket
334 W. Main
Fredericksburg, TX 78624
(512) 997-4533 Rubye Hallford

Pecan Producers, Inc.
P.O. Box 1301, Corsicana, TX 75110
(214) 872-1337 Elton Raney

Pecan Shed
Highway 79, Byers, TX 76357
(817) 544-2253 Molly Montz

Pecan Valley Nut Company, Inc.
P.O. Box 854, Stephenville, TX 76401
(817) 965-5031 Doyle Welch

Pedernales Valley Orchard & Farms
Rt. 2, Box 154
Fredericksburg, TX 78624
(512) 997-6723 David White

Pedro Gatos Salsa, Inc.
1712 W. 29th St. #2, Austin, TX 78703
(512) 472-2040 Pete Katz

Pedro's Tamales
· P.O. Box 3571, Lubbock, TX 79452
(806) 745-9531 Pete Hale

Perry Products
Rt. 2, Box 145, Giddings, TX 78942
(409) 542-5009 G. Allen Perry

Pet, Inc., Old El Paso Foods
400 S. 4th Street, St. Louis, MO 63102
(314) 622-6181 Patricia Christensen

Pheasant Ridge Winery
Rt. 3, Box 191, Lubbock, TX 79401
(806) 746-6033 Charles R. Cox

Picosos Peanut Co., Inc.
P.O. Box 584, Helotes, TX 78023
(512) 695-8727 Jimmie Gennero

Piney Woods Country Wines
3408 Willow Drive, Orange, TX 77630
(409) 883-5408 Alfred J. Flies

Pioneer Flour Mills
P.O. Box 118, San Antonio, TX 78291
(512) 227-1401 Patrick D. Keenan

Pipecreek Texas Bullcorn
11726 Santa Cruz, Austin, TX 78759
(512) 345-1472 Pat Foy

Plainview Produce, Inc.
P.O. Box 818, Plainview, TX 79073
(806) 293-9541 Rusty Ingram

Plantation Foods, Inc.
P.O. Box 20788, Waco, TX 76702
(817) 799-6211 Trudi Hicks

Plantation Pines Berry Farm
Rt. 22, Box 266, Tyler, TX 75704
(214) 592-2041 Clinton Wiggins

Poor Farm, The
Rt. 4, Box 280, Wichita Falls, TX 76301
(817) 544-2442 David M. Comstock

Preston Trail Winery
6420 Camille Ave., Dallas, TX 75252
(214) 867-8024 Thomas J. Greaves

Primarily Barbecue
Rt. 1, Box 250, Moulton, TX 77975
(512) 596-7278 Morris O'Tyson

Producer Perfect Beef
Box 158, Valley Mills, TX 76689
(817) 932-6151 W. F. Barrett

Progressive Groves, Inc.
P.O. Box 87, Weslaco, TX 78596
(512) 968-9521 W. C. Chuck Schneider

Purity Ice Cream Mfgr.
1202 Post Office St.
Galveston, TX 77550
(409) 765-6661 Jack H. King

Quality Peanut Warehouses, Inc.
P.O. Box 67, Lexington, TX 78947
(409) 773-2610 Phillip D. McCall

Quality Texas Products, Inc.
P.O. Box 355, Bryson, TX 76027
(817) 392-5555 Parky Parkinson

R & B Quail Farm
Star Route 4, BOX 274
Blanco, TX 78606
(512) 833-5194 J. M. Buck

Ramage Farms
Route 1, Box 111, Hooks, TX 75561
(214) 547-6187 Barton H. Ramage

Ranch House Meat Co.
Box 855 (303 San Saba)
Menard, TX 76859
(915) 396-2101 Max L. Stabel

Rayner Packing Co.
P.O. Box 21202, Houston, TX 77226
(713) 228-9557 Allan J. Reitzer

Reba's Country Cupboard
P.O. Box 80, Washington, TX 77880
(409) 878-2112 Reba Corley

Red Eye Company
P.O. Box 325, Florence, TX 76527
(817) 793-2799 John A. Fenoglio, II

Reinauer & Sons, Inc., E. C.
P.O. Box 1637, Hereford, TX 79045
(806) 276-5291 E. C. Reinauer

Rex & Johnnie's Little Acre
Route 1, Box 184
Bridgeport, TX 76026
(817) 683-2370 Rex D. Bearden

Rhew Peach Orchard
Rt. 5, Box 247, Floresville, TX 78114
(512) 393-6022 Frank Rhew

Richards Horticulture
P.O. Box 5622, Midland, TX 79704
(915) 686-0643 Guy Richards

Richland Beverage Corp.
7557 Rambler Rd., #1326
Dallas, TX 75231
(214) 891-5500 Cathy Zelzer

Richter Wine Group, Inc.
1403 W. 6th St., Austin, TX 78703
(512) 476-5772 Monet Stalle

Rico Products
621 S. Flores, San Antonio, TX 78204
(512) 222-1415 R. A. Ferber

Riddick Farms
Route 2, Box 176, Jasper, TX 75951
(409) 384-7877 William L. Riddick

Riker Farm
Box 18, Anton, TX 79313
(806) 997-4108 William C. Riker

Roaring Springs Jam Factory
P.O. Box 248
Roaring Springs, TX 79256
(806) 348-7253 Wesley Day

Ruiz Tamale & Tortilla Factory
422 14th & Marguerite
Corpus Christi, TX 78401
(512) 888-6177 Grace Hernandez

Russell Vineyards
HC-31, Box F, Pecan Road
Gardendale, TX 79758
(915) 563-1657 Thomas W. Russell

Ruthie's Chip Corporation
P.O. Box 12163, Dallas, TX 75225
(214) 373-3183 Pamela Ann Melton

S & D Holmes Smokehouse, Inc.
913 Crabb River Road
Richmond, TX 77469
(713) 342-3740 Stephen A. Holmes

Sadler's Bar-B-Que Sales, Inc.
P.O. Box 1088, Henderson, TX 75652
(214) 657-5581 Jim Sweeny

Sam Kane Beef Processors, Inc.
P.O. Box 9254
Corpus Christi, TX 78469
(512) 289-9000 Jerry Kane

San Antonio Packing Co.
P.O. Box 7265, San Antonio, TX 78207
(512) 224-5441 Richard H. Reyes

San Antonio River Mill
129 East Guenther Street
San Antonio, TX 78204
(512) 227-4821 Scott Anderson

San Saba Pecan, Inc.
2803 W. Wallace, San Saba, TX 76877
(915) 372-5727 R. D. Buddy Adams

Sanchez Creek Vineyards
DSR Box 30-4, Weatherford, TX 76086
(817) 594-6884 Ron Wetherington

Sand Pit Enterprises, Inc.
Box 10, New Baden, TX 77870
(409) 828-4767 L. K. DeZavala

Sandwoods Farm
Rt. 4, Box 248, Caldwell, TX 77836
(409) 535-4022 Randie M. Cook

Sandy Foot Farm
Route 5, Box 588
Livingston, TX 77351
(409) 327-2744 Mary W. Smith

Sandy Hill Farm
P.O. Box 6483, Tyler, TX 75711
(214) 561-5500 William Watson

Segovia Mexican Candy
P.O. Box 1943, Brenham, TX 77833
(713) 392-0282 J. Robert Chappell

Sem-Tex Produce
Box 608, Seminole, TX 79360
(915) 758-9251 R. E. Messer

Senor Pepe, Inc.
1414 N. Jacinto
San Antonio, TX 78207
(512) 735-6163 Rogue R. Garcia

Serendipity Of The Valley
P.O. Box 787, Lake Jackson, TX 77566
(409) 297-2367 Marty Tyson

Serloin Shops Of Stephenville, Inc.
P.O. Box 5, Stephenville, TX 76401
(817) 968-4177 Oren Webb

Sklar's Frozen Food Center, Inc.
2014 N. Richmond Rd.
Wharton, TX 77488
(409) 532-4272 Lillie D. Sklar

Skweezins Corporation
14651 Dallas Parkway, #119
Dallas, TX 75240
(214) 387-3847 John C. Rogers

Sky Line Growers
HCR #2, Box 6321
Pipe Creek, TX 78063
(512) 535-4893 Shawn L. Byron

Smith's Peach Farm
Rt. 1, Box 46, Pittsburg, TX 75686
(214) 856-6488 John E. Smith

Smokemaster Products, Inc.
P.O. Box 202029, Dallas, TX 75220
(214) 350-1384 Rozan Williams

Smokey Denmark Sausage Co.
3505 East 5th, Austin, TX 78702
(512) 385-0718 Don Kuker

Snacks and Candies, Inc.
P.O. Box 1342, Laredo, TX 78041
(512) 722-5588 Manuel Villegas

Sonja's Internat'l. Confections
P.O. Box 18369
Corpus Christi, TX 78418
(512) 937-4731 Sonja Silvertooth

Soupcon Corporation
2313 West Belt North #131
Houston, TX 77043
(713) 464-6674 Diane Langwith

South Texas Mesquite Corp.
20111 Hwy. 97 West
Jourdanton, TX 78026
(512) 769-2550 Bobby House

South Texas Spice Co., Inc.
7431-B Reindeer Trail
San Antonio, TX 78238
(512) 684-6239 Chris Cooley

Southern Blues Farm
250 S. Sunset, Vidor, TX 77662
(409) 768-1284 H. D. Self

Southern Gold Honey Co.
3015 Brown Road, Vidor, TX 77662
(409) 768-1645 Kenneth Horn

Southwest Citrus, Inc.
11020 Old Katy Rd., #214
Houston, TX 77043
(713) 465-1481 Ray E. Basford

Spear Orchard
Star Rt. 1, Box 9, Fischer, TX 78623
(512) 935-2693 Homer Spear

Specialty Process Corp.
1350 S. Industrial, Dallas, TX 75207
(214) 426-0204 B. W. Alford

Spoetzl Brewery, Inc.
603 Brewery Street, Shiner, TX 77984
(512) 594-3852 George Korknas

Spring River Farm
1616 Old Martindale Rd.
San Marcos, TX 78666
(512) 353-2780 R. Thomas

Ste. Genevieve Vineyards
P.O. Box 717, Ft. Stockton, TX 79735
(915) 395-2417 Bill Pauli

Sterling Orchards
P.O. Box 4, Clayton, TX 75637
(214) 693-4109 Charles Davis

Sunbelt America
P.O. Box 789, Littlefield, TX 79339
(806) 385-4468 Tommy Thrash

Sunday House Foods, Inc.
P.O. Box 818
Fredericksburg, TX 78624
(512) 997-2136 P. J. Crane

Sundor Corp.
P.O. Box 327, Weslaco, TX 78596
(512) 968-2141 Fran Graham

Sunrise Ranch
Rt. 3, Box 39P, Liberty Hill, TX 78642
(512) 778-6730 John T. Baker

Sunset Vineyard & Nursery
Route 1, Box 535, Sunset, TX 76270
(817) 845-2821 Robert B. Hart, Jr.

Superior Dairies
600 East First, Austin, TX 78701
(512) 476-0683 M. J. Adamson

Supreme Products, Inc.
P.O. Box 3786, McAllen, TX 78502
(512) 686-1344 Hector J. Villarreal

Swiss Pride Dairies
P.O. Box 310277
New Braunfels, TX 78130
(512) 625-7543 Norvin Wetz

Sysco Food Services
535 Portwall, Houston, TX 77220
(713) 672-8080 Richard A. Ewert

Talk O' Texas Brands, Inc.
P.O. Box 2607
Grand Prairie, TX 75053
(214) 642-5700 Lindy Chandler

Tangram Nursery
Route 1, Box 155, Maxwell, TX 78656
(512) 396-0667 Harlan Shoulders

Taormina Co.
P.O. Box 965, Donna, TX 78537
(512) 464-3328 Frank A. Taormina

Tejano Products
139 Chelsea, El Paso, TX 79905
(915) 778-3111 C. Ruiz

Tejas Specialties
301 East Centre
Federicksburg, TX 78624
(512) 997-2583 Cathryn H. Hensell

Tejas Vineyard & Winery
P.O. Box 92, Mesquite, TX 75149
(214) 285-3644 Donald Frank

Tekita House Foods, Inc.
7024 Alameda Ave., El Paso, TX 79915
(915) 778-5481 Joe Talamantes

TexaFrance/Custom Catering
815-A Brazos Street, Austin, TX 78701
(512) 479-0888 David Griswald

Texas American Cookie Co.
P.O. Box 810333, Houston, TX 77281
(713) 780-3600 Frank Midgett

Texas Bee Company-Varsel Apiaries
P.O. Box 1272, Spring, TX 77383
(713) 376-5343 Mark W. Varsel

Texas Bess
4801 Bratcher, Fort Worth, TX 76119
(817) 536-1228 Sheila K. Williams

Texas Best Produce
Box 733, Premont, TX 78375
(512) 348-3039 Roel Gonzales

Texas Blueberry Marketing Group
Rt. 2, Box 169, LaRue, TX 75770
(214) 675-4022 Donald Cawthon

Texas Blueberry Plantation
Rt. 7, Box 87, Reins Road
Beaumont, TX 77706
(409) 753-2890 John H. Kerr

Texas Citrus Exchange
P.O. Box 793, Mission, TX 78572
(512) 585-8336 Jim Phillips

Texas Crawfish Farmers Association
P.O. Box 2735, Orange, TX 77631
(409) 883-7740 Joe Heinen

Texas Duet
P.O. Box 26529, Austin, TX 78755
(512) 343-0116 Suzy Platt

Texas Fresh
706 North Park Circle
Cedar Park, TX 78613
(512) 258-9784 Dale Jolly

Texas Fruit Baskets
2311 Thornton, Austin, TX 78704
(512) 445-0627 Lois Goodman

Texas Honey Co-Op Inc.
9114 Walhalla, San Antonio, TX 78221
(512) 927-9781 Richard W. Razvillas

Texas Jellies
Box 13496, Austin, TX 78711
(512) 445-6714 Melinda Cullinan

Texas Natural Gifts Honey Co.
401 Cherry Creek, Dayton, TX 77535
(409) 258-3034 T. Ray Chancey

Texas Original Mesquite Jelly
102 Travis Street
Port Lavaca, TX 77979
(512) 552-9419 Melody Chatelle

Texas Pecan & Gourmet Co.
P.O. Box 1432, San Angelo, TX 76902
(915) 653-6841 Wade B. Simpson

Texas Prairie, Inc.
1716 15th Place, Plano, TX 75074
(214) 423-3241 Dave Fondren

Texas Vineyards Inc.
P.O. Box 33, Ivanhoe, TX 75447
(214) 424-1976 Ron UPton

Texas Western Beef
P.O. Box 2989, Spring, TX 77383
(713) 376-0304 John W. Bellinger

Texas Wild Game Cooperative
P.O. Box 530, Ingram, TX 78025
(512) 367-5875 D. M. Hughes

Texas Ya-Hoo Cake Co.
2160 I-30 East, Rockwall, TX 75087
(214) 722-5624 Todd C. Coppic

Texham, Inc.
12815 Mula Lane, Stafford, TX 77477
(713) 495-2053 Armando Solorzano

Textray
1100 W. Koenig Lane
Austin, TX 78756
(512) 458-3291 Nicholas J. Juried

Thompson Farms, Inc.
10940 Laureate Dr., Suite 8310
San Antonio, TX 78249
(512) 697-3104 Otis Sumlin

Traylor Farms, Inc.
Rt. 1, Box 140, Naples, TX 75568
(214) 884-2611 Jan Traylor Ragland

Triple C Meats
P.O. Box 467, Devine, TX 78016
(512) 663-3636 Kenneth Cox

Truly Delicious Candies
P.O. Box 1422, Gladewater, TX 75647
(214) 845-2067 Carolyn Guthrie

Tucker's Farm & Craft
Rt. 4, Box 281, Wichita Falls, TX 76301
(817) 544-2455 Deloris Tucker

Tule Creek Apiary
Rt. 2, 739 North Dallas
Tulia, TX 79088
(806) 995-3771 Kenneth Patton

Twelve Oaks
Rt. 3, Box 264A, Hillsboro, TX 76645
(817) 582-2815 Bruce Gillespie

Tyler Candy Co., Inc.
P.O. Box 6556, Tyler, TX 75701
(214) 561-3046 Bryan Carey

Underwood's Fine Foods
310 E. Main, Waxahachie, TX 75165
(214) 840-8841 Gloria Brown

Union Slaughter, Inc.
1000 Plaza Avenue, Del Rio, TX 78840
(512) 775-7461 Oscar San Miguel

Uvalde Meat Processing
508 South Wood St., Uvalde, TX 78801
(512) 278-6247 Evelyn Shaw

Val Verde Winery
139 Hudson Drive, Del Rio, TX 78840
(512) 775-9714 Susan Ayres

Valentine Co., Inc.
305 W. Bluff, Woodville, TX 75979
(409) 283-2495 James A. Knecht

Valley Farmers Co-op
Rt. 1, Box 44-4, San Juan, TX 78589
(512) 787-0823 Julio Castilleja

Valley Wholesale Meat Co. Inc.
1000 E. Frontage Rd., Alamo, TX 78516
(512) 787-2553 Robert Cantu

Valley Wholesale Meat Co. Inc. II
P.O. Box 119, Alamo, TX 78516
(512) 380-0004 Jose Cantu

Van De Walle Farms, Inc.
5310 Old Hwy. 90W
San Antonio, TX 78227
(512) 436-5551 Larry Friesenhahn

Vanco Products Co., Inc.
2916 Delafield, Houston, TX 77023
(713) 921-0234 Bobby Nelson

Vandervoort Dairy Foods Co.
900 South Main St.
Fort Worth, TX 76104
(817) 332-7551 Bob Ellis

Weaver & Sons
Rt. 1, Box 24, Navasota, TX 77868
(409) 825-7714 Morris Weaver

Weaver Apiaries, Inc.
Route 1, Box 256, Navasota, TX 77868
(409) 825-3367 Roy S. Weaver, Jr.

Webb's Candy Co.
P.O. Box 634, Boerne, TX 78006
(512) 249-3284 Joyce Webb

Weidenfeller Trading Co.
208 W. Schubert
Fredericksburg, TX 78624
(512) 997-2248 J. P. Weidenfeller

West Brand, Inc.
901 Main St., #4600, Dallas, TX 75202
(214) 872-5245 Dianne W. Short

Westside Orchard
Rt. 4, Box 283, Wichita Falls, TX 76301
(817) 544-2447 E. D. Chitwood

Wimberley Valley Wines, Inc.
Fredericksburg Rt. Box 634
Harper, TX 77301
(512) 669-2440 Charles L. Hereford

Winn's Good Cooking
P.O. Box 1306, Wylie, TX 75098
(214) 442-6775 Winn McClure

Wolf Brand Products
2626 Cole Ave., #950
Dallas, TX 75204
(214) 871-7530 Lawrence E. Kurzius

Woodrum Produce
213 Forrest Lane, Fruitvale, TX 75127
(214) 963-3675 Jimmy L. Woodrum

Woody's Meats, Inc.
1102 S. Virginia, Terrell, TX 75160
(214) 563-1469 O. W. Wurdeman

Yoakum Packing Co.
Box 192, Yoakum, TX 77995
(512) 293-3541 C. R. Reed

Young's Greenhouses
Rt. 4, Box 276, Wichita Falls, TX 76301
(817) 544-2417 J. Cooper Young

Young's Home Orchard
Rt. 4, Box 299, Wichita Falls, TX 76301
(817) 544-2449 J. B. Young, Jr.

Youngblood Honey, Inc.
1216 E. Alabama St.
Pearsall, TX 78061
(512) 334-4430 Elbert E.
Youngblood, Sr.

Zero Food Locker
P.O. Box 518, Bridgeport, TX 76026
(817) 683-2362 Ocie Vest

Zeys Of Texas
P.O. Box 1048, 701 Bryan
Mission, TX 78572
(512) 585-8383 J. Eric Zey

Zita's
1505-A Summer Creek Dr.
Austin, TX 78704
(512) 442-8604 Mandy Wright

LOGOS OF TASTE OF TEXAS COMPANIES
WHOSE RECIPES ARE IN THE COOKBOOK

Adams Extract Co.

Allen Canning Co.

Adkins Seasoning Co.

Ambrosia Orchards

Specialty Process Corp.

Amigos Canning Co., Inc.

Aldus Co.

Angel Craft, Inc.

Artesia Waters, Inc.

Bolner's Fiesta Products, Inc.

BELLVILLE
TORTILLA CHIP

Bellville Potato Chip Factory

B3R Country Meats, Inc.

B3R Country Meats, Inc.

Brazos Valley Orchards

Texas Citrus Exchange

Brockett-Tyree Farms

Blackland Apiaries Honey

Blueberry Patch

Caliente Chili, Inc.

Burrus Milling, Dept. of Cargill

Carlton Food Products, Inc.

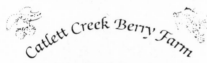

Catlett Creek Berry Farm

Cedar Mountain Buffalo Company

Chateau Montgolfier Vineyards

Chef A. Joseph Products, Inc.

Collin Street Bakery

Cox's Relish Co., Inc.

Das Peach Haus

Dickie Davis Sweet & Hot

Doguet Rice Milling Co.

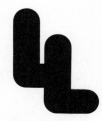

Double L Ranch, The

E & B Peach Orchard

Eastex Farms

Energy Sprouts, Inc.

Fall Creek Vineyards

Farms Of Texas

Fincastle Nursery & Farms

Frog House, The

Gandy's Dairies, Inc.

IMPERIAL SUGAR

Imperial Sugar Co.

Guadalupe Valley Winery

Janet's Own Home Sweet Home

Hell On The Red, Inc.

Hill Country Spring Water Of TX

Lantana Seasoning

La Martinique
Restaurant Dressing

Pace Foods, Inc.

Weaver & Sons

Laxson Provision Co.

Hubbell & Sons Food Products, Inc.

Lazy Susan, Inc.

Moyer Texas Champagne Co.

Lone Star Bakery, Inc.

Mr. Bar-B-Q, Inc.

Millie's Kountry Kitchen

Neal's Cookies

Miss Mary's Fine Foods

Pace Foods, Inc.

Monterey House, Inc.

Pecan Valley Nut Company, Inc.

PIONEER

Pioneer Flour Mills

Specialty Process Corp.

Primarily Barbecue

O. B. Macaroni Co.

Sandy Hill Farm

Rico Products

San Antonio River Mill

Roaring Springs Jam Factory

Serendipity Of The Valley

Soupcon Corporation

Pace Foods, Inc.

South Texas Spice Co., Inc.

TexaFrance/Custom Catering

Specialty Process Corp.

Texas Crawfish Farmers Association

Superior Dairies

Texas Duet

Talk O' Texas Brands, Inc.

Texas Pecan & Gourmet Co.

Texas Western Beef

Underwood's Fine Foods

Vanco Products Co., Inc.

Van De Walle Farms, Inc.

West Brand, Inc.

Westside Orchard

Whole Foods

Wimberley Valley Wines, Inc.

Woody's Meats, Inc.

Mickle, Inc.

Youngblood Honey, Inc.

Set Your TEXAS TABLE
with a COOKBOOK from
EAKIN PRESS

Additional copies of our TASTE OF TEXAS COOKBOOK may be purchased at your local food store or book store, or it you wish you may order copies of this or any of our cookbooks from Eakin Press, using the convenient order form below. The hardback edition of the TASTE OF TEXAS COOKBOOK is $10.95.

Quantity	Book Title	Price

Charge my
☐ **VISA**   ☐ Payment enclosed
☐ **MasterCard**

Account

Exp. Date_____ Tel. #_____

Signature_____

Subtotal _____

Postage and Handling _____

Texas Sales Tax _____

Total _____

EAKIN PUBLICATIONS, INC.
P.O. Box 23069   Austin, Texas 78735
Phone (512) 288-1771

Cooking With Pecans
By Terry Scott Bertling

Huntsville newspaper editor Terry Scott Bertling shows how versatile the pecan is in the kitchen in her new *Cooking With Pecans*. Her several hundred recipes are a collection of old-time Texas with a generous sprinkling of new selections. She provides pecan recipes for appetizers and snacks, salads, main dishes, side dishes, desserts and pies, and, of course, candies and cookies. $5^{1}/_{2}$ x $8^{1}/_{2}$, 112 pages, photos, index.
Hardback, ISBN 574-7 .... **$11.95**

The First Texas Cookbook
**Special Sesquicentennial
Collector's Edition**

A handsome reprint of the 1883 original of recipes from great-grandmother's kitchen collected by the ladies of the First Presbyterian Church of Houston. Original Texana with colorful words and phrases (such as yelk, instead of yolk), but also no-nonsense recipes for today's cooks. Forewords by David Wade and Mary Faulk Koock. 6 x 9, 212 pages, more than 800 recipes, collector's edition.
ISBN 518-6 .... **$12.95**

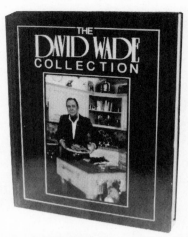

The David Wade Collection
By David Wade

For thirty-six years, David Wade has been America's premier gourmet cook and television and radio personality. The country has fallen in love with this deep-voiced, flamboyant and always sophisticated chef. He whips up delectable dishes fit for kings while nattily attired in his trademark ascot and navy blazer. He chats with famous guests and never misses a beat or looks less than elegant. Today he makes his home in Tyler, Texas, and televises many of his programs from his specially designed kitchen. **9 x 9, 196 pages, elegant hardback edition, eight-page color insert with photographs of some of the author's most famous recipes. ISBN 554-2** **$19.95**

Cooking on a Wood Stove
By Doris McLaughlin

Cooking on a Wood Stove is more than a cookbook of old fashioned recipes — it is a short course in the art of "old-timey" cookery. The author was born and raised on a piney woods farm at Latexo near Crockett in East Texas. 5$^1/_2$ x 8$^1/_2$, 200 pages.
Paperback, ISBN 396-5 .... **$9.95**

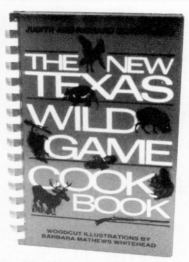

The New Texas Wild Game Cookbook
By Judith and Richard Morehead

More nutritious than domestic meat, higher in protein, lower in fat, higher in fiber, lower in sodium . . . This is a theme of *The New Texas Wild Game Cookbook*. The Moreheads and other gourmet cooks have discovered what many continental chefs already knew — game dishes, properly prepared, are delicious. The recipes, with minor exceptions, all have been kitchen-tested by the authors and their friends. They range from venison, dove, quail, pheasant, turkey, waterfowl, and imported sheep to javelina, armadillo, and 'possum. The Moreheads make their home in Austin. $5^3/_4$ x $8^3/_4$, spiral binding, 104 pages. **ISBN 526-7 .... $9.95**

South Texas Mexican Cookbook
By Lucy Garza

This delightful cookbook is straight from the *cocina* of a South Texas traditional Mexican home. Don't expect the regular fare of restaurants specializing in "Mexican" food, but if you want a nostalgic trip down memory lane and tidbits to tantalize even the most avid gourmet, try some of Lucy Garza's down-home recipes. $5^1/_2$ x $8^1/_2$, spiral binding, 96 pages, original art. **ISBN 344-2 ...... $9.95**